SECRET WISCONSIN

A Guide to the Weird, Wonderful, and Obscure

I0809029

Tom Manus and Kristi Flick Manus

REEDY PRESS

Reedy Press
PO Box 5131
St. Louis, MO 63139
www.reedypress.com

Library of Congress Control Number: 2023938776
ISBN: 9781681064949

Design by Jill Halpin

Unless otherwise indicated, all photos are courtesy of the authors or in the public domain.

Printed in the United States of America
26 27 5 4

To Tim, throughout your life, remain in the quiet solitude of the forests and the trees where you can listen for a casual reply. Always remember to find the sanctuary found in majestic mountain tops. Look down to see the silver clouds below and the tranquility of clear blue mountain lakes. Look way beyond the blue of what you can see to find all that this life can be.

Yesterday's Sign Park
Photo courtesy of Antigo/Langlade County Chamber of Commerce

CONTENTS

Gravity Hill

INTRODUCTION

Wisconsin has unique stories that must be told. It has been a joy for us to research and share about our home state. Our hope is that *Secret Wisconsin* inspires you to dig deeper where you live and find new areas to explore on your next road trip. There are many things about Wisconsin that you may already know. Like how we have more lakes than our neighbors to the west, and how anglers come to Wisconsin for world-class fishing. Especially for musky, the fish of 10,000 casts. But, we tell you where to visit the world's largest musky fish hatchery and about a unique museum nearby dedicated to canoes. Sure, we live in "America's Dairyland," but Wisconsin is the only place on earth, other than Switzerland, where a Master Cheesemaker certificate can be obtained. This grueling program is often referred to as a PhD in cheese. Over the years, musicians flocked to the state to perform, many in small-town venues. Elvis, Buddy Holly, Otis Redding, and Johnny Cash, to name a few. Because of one gruesome incident, an opening band had to change its name, then became a household name in the '80s.

In addition to delightful cities and small towns, the entire state offers excellent outdoor experiences for making memories. Our son learned to fish and camp from his grandpa in the Northwoods. Often, he has been our guide by telling us about places off the beaten path they visited together. It seems like they left no rock unturned.

This same sense of discovery runs in our family. It can be described in this partial quote by Thomas Jefferson to Meriwether Lewis, "The object of your mission is to explore..." Whether you are a lifelong Wisconsinite or new to the state, *Secret Wisconsin* is for you. Use it as a tourist guide for discovering the nooks and crannies of the state. Carry on Wisconsin's road trip culture. Go explore. Make memories.

WELCOME TO CLEVELAND

Is this Cleveland or Milwaukee?

What would cause a guy to take a bucket of paint onto his roof on a random Wednesday afternoon and spell out “Welcome to Cleveland” in six-foot white letters? You might think this was merely eccentric until you realized that the man resides in Milwaukee. Unfortunately for some, Mark Gubin was bored one afternoon and came up with the plan in 1978. His photography studio and home, located in an old theater on Delaware Street, is directly below the flight path of runway 19 at the Milwaukee Mitchell International Airport. Most of the flights that land in Milwaukee make their approach over Lake Michigan and fly right over his sign.

You can imagine the confusion this sign causes aboard inbound flights. Passengers have seen the “Welcome to Cleveland” sign for decades and assumed their pilot has taken a wrong turn or they have somehow gotten on an incorrect flight. On one regular flight, the pilot announced that the sign was wrong to avoid panic or confusion. The city council president once sent a letter informing Gubin that the welcome sign was causing outrage and panic in the sky for some passengers. Still, he was never asked to remove it.

WELCOME TO CLEVELAND

WHAT: “Welcome to Cleveland” rooftop sign

WHERE: 2893 S Delaware Ave., Milwaukee (not Cleveland)

COST: Free, but you may need to book a flight arriving in Milwaukee to see it

PRO TIP: The best way to see the sign is from the air. So next time you fly into Milwaukee, remember to look out the left-side window. If you see the “Welcome to Cleveland” sign, you are right where you are supposed to be—in Milwaukee.

On approaching Milwaukee International Airport, don't be confused by the Welcome to Cleveland sign. Photo courtesy of Tim Manus Photography

The sign is still there today to welcome passengers. We flew a drone over the sign, and it looked freshly painted and in better condition than the roof that it was painted on.

Brad Heasman in Sidney, Australia, tried to replicate the prank and painted a "Welcome to Perth" sign on the roof of his business in 2021.

TRAVELING EGG ROLLS

Why do egg rolls travel in coolers?

Over 100 years ago, in November 1922, the Cozy Inn opened in downtown Janesville. The acclaimed eatery is the oldest Chinese restaurant in Wisconsin and the second-oldest Chinese restaurant in America in business at the same location. The Cozy Inn is located on the second floor, above an Irish pub. Below its classic neon sign you can walk up a flight of stairs for a dining experience in one of Wisconsin's best-kept secrets.

Tom Wong grew up in Chinese restaurants. His mother was a highly acclaimed chef in Milwaukee but wanted to open her own business. She bought the Cozy Inn in 1974, and it has been in the family since. Now, Tom focuses on cooking while his wife, Amanda, runs the operation. Since opening in 1922, chop suey and chow mein have been staples on the menu, but egg rolls are the most popular offering. However, the secret family egg roll recipe takes two days to prepare. Orders are brought to tables in stainless-steel pedestal dishes like they were 50 years ago. Along with cooking remarkable cuisine, the secret of the Cozy Inn's enduring success is the family's extraordinary devotion to treating customers like close friends. For example, for customers who can't climb the stairs, Amanda meets them on the sidewalk.

The restaurant is located above an Irish pub. Photo courtesy of Janesville CVB

The Cozy Inn has been a Chinese restaurant for over 100 years. Photo courtesy of Janesville CVB

COZY INN CHINESE RESTAURANT

WHAT: Iconic restaurant that has been in business for over 100 years

WHERE: 214 W Milwaukee St., Janesville

COST: Legendary egg rolls are $2.35

PRO TIP: Order egg rolls. Many former Janesville residents call days ahead to order large quantities to take home in coolers.

Customers can eat in original 1922 round wood booths with head-high backrests, but vintage curtains used at the entry are no longer installed. There's also an old wood coin telephone booth from the same year. Customers take photos inside pretending to use the black rotary dial phone, and some have private cell phone conversations inside because of its classic soundproofing. Step back in time at the Cozy Inn.

Tom Wong's father, a mariner en route to his next job, was one of six Chinese survivors of the *Titanic*. A recent documentary named *The Six*, by executive producer James Cameron, was made about their rescue.

THE *BOY WITH THE LEAKING BOOT*

Why does the *Boy with the Leaking Boot* disappear from August to May?

Driving down US 51 in Stevens Point, you pass a four-foot-tall sculpture of a young boy holding a leaky boot that dribbles water into a cement pool—but only from May through August. Stevens Point is home to one of an estimated 25 leaking-boot-boy statues left in the country.

The *Boy with the Leaking Boot* water fountain was purchased via mail order from the J. L. Mott Iron Works Company in New York City. The statue arrived in Stevens Point in 1895 and was placed in the center of town as a drinking fountain. The fountain was in service until 1914. Then, the figure was in dismal condition and was taken down. Along came the firemen to the rescue. The boy was found in a nearby field by two firefighters and was placed in the flower bed of the North Side Fire Station, where he stood until 1967, when he was moved to the basement. Finally, in July 1975, the boy was again repaired and was given a new place to stand, thanks to the firefighters and local residents.

Stevens Point is a college town, and with it come antics. The *Boy with the Leaking Boot* has been vandalized, stolen, decapitated, and had its legs broken on different occasions. The poor boy was constantly in need of repair. The caretakers of the statue, the firefighters

LEAKY BOOT FOUNTAIN

WHAT: The *Boy with the Leaking Boot* fountain

WHERE: Stevens Point Fire Department Headquarters, 1701 Franklin St., Stevens Point

COST: Free

PRO TIP: Be sure to visit the *Boy with the Leaking Boot* from May through August. The boy is taken down and stored as soon as the college students arrive for the school season.

Hidden during most of the year, summer is the best time to see the statue.

at Fire Station No. 1, decided to put the figure away during the school year to deter vandalism. A fiberglass replica of the statue has also been created, with the original figure stored in the basement. Hopefully, the *Boy with the Leaking Boot* will continue to adorn the fountain in front of Fire Station No. 1 along US 51 in Stevens Point forever.

The original name of the statue was *The Unfortunate Boy*, a Civil War child who used his boot to carry water to dying soldiers.

COLA MUSEUM

What is golden cola?

Tiny suspended citrus pieces float throughout the nation's first golden cola. Sun Drop, a deep-rooted favorite of Southerners, has been a popular carbonated drink since the 1950s, when horizontally shaped drink machines kept glass bottles ice cold. Chilled water dripped down the side when customers opened the metal top-sliding doors to take a bottle out. Towels hung from the cooler's end to wipe them dry. Yes, that's the best way to enjoy Sun Drop, straight from green glass bottles pulled from old-fashioned drink machines.

Charles Lazier, a beverage concentrate salesman, took his Sun Drop recipe from St. Louis to Twig's bottling factory in Shawano for distribution. Soon after, kids anticipated drinking the new beverage flavor on their annual summer trip up north. Just as important as fishing poles and inner tubes, the drink became a cult favorite. Parents fished, often until dusk, as the resort's kid clientele played while impatiently waiting on shore for the hum of boat motors to arrive. At night, adults sat at the bar, but kids lined their bottles of Sun Drop next to their bar, a pinball machine.

Whether these images bring back good memories or you're a newcomer to the drink, the Twig's Sun Drop University

---

Twig's makes Sun Drop with real sugar, not corn syrup. Fifty-pound bags of sugar are mixed with every batch. Most bottling companies make Sun Drop with corn syrup.

Sun Drop, still bottled in glass bottles today.

Museum is fun. Memorabilia fills each room floor to ceiling, but a classic flatbed truck loaded with wooden cases of glass Sun Drop bottles stands out. In one room, vintage drink machines line one wall, while another is dedicated to Dale Earnhardt's day as a promoter. Metal Sun Drop antique signs abound everywhere. Sit in green, hand-shaped chairs and enjoy free samples at the tasting bar before visiting a well-stocked gift shop. After touring the working warehouse you can view some fine art—like a portrait of Mona Lisa holding a Sun Drop, or Kramer from the hit television show *Seinfeld* posing in a suit with a Sun Drop chest emblem.

TWIG'S SUN DROP UNIVERSITY MUSEUM

WHAT: Museum dedicated to the first golden cola

WHERE: 920 S Franklin St., Shawano

COST: Free

PRO TIP: If you enjoy an old-fashioned, add a twist by making it with Sun Drop.

DESIGNED WHITE ELEPHANT

Where does architecture meet science?

If you catch the scent of a Glade air freshener or avoid a swarm of mosquitoes thanks to Off, you can thank Frank Lloyd Wright. In 1950, he built the SC Johnson Research Tower at the company's headquarters in Racine, Wisconsin. The research tower was home to the invention of many of the company's essential products.

WHITE ELEPHANT BUILDING

WHAT: SC Johnson Research Tower

WHERE: 1525 Howe St., Racine

COST: Free

PRO TIP: Tours are given of the administration building and the research tower. Please note that no indoor photos or videos may be taken on tours. Exterior photos are encouraged.

The tower, rising 153 feet above the ground, is one of the tallest buildings ever built on a cantilever principle. The tower is 40 feet across, yet at ground level it's supported by a base only 13 feet across at its narrowest point. As a result, the building almost seems to be hanging in the air. The floors are alternating square and round mezzanine levels that make up the interior. A core in the center of the building houses the elevators, stairway, and restrooms. The core descends 54 feet into the ground to provide stability. The design is similar to that of a tree and its root system.

After being closed for longer than it was open, in 2013, after an extensive restoration, the research tower was again opened, but not for research and development.

SC Johnson's research and development department called the research tower home from 1950 to 1982. However, in 1982 new building codes required a fire escape to be added to the outside of the tower, or it would have to be closed. SC Johnson decided to close the historic building to protect Frank Lloyd Wright's sleek design.

Frank Lloyd Wright designed the building.

HOW A LONG SPEECH SAVED A PRESIDENT'S LIFE

How fit is a bull moose?

In 1912, Theodore Roosevelt was running for yet another term as president. He had already served as the 26th president from 1901 to 1909. When he entered the race, he declared himself as fit as a bull moose and thus caused his new progressive party to be called the Bull Moose Party.

On October 14, 1912, President Roosevelt was in Milwaukee for a campaign stop. He had just finished eating dinner at Hotel Gilpatrick on the corner of Third and Kilbourn Street and was going to give his stump speech. Roosevelt stood up in the car's back seat, and while he waved his hat at the crowd, John Schrank shot him in the chest from only five feet away with a .32 caliber bullet. The shot should have killed the president, but the bullet was slowed by the thick metal eyeglass case and his folded 50-page speech in his pocket. The bullet entered his chest near the rib cage and became lodged.

Being the bull moose he was, Roosevelt proceeded to the Milwaukee Auditorium instead of the hospital, hell-bent on giving the speech to those who were waiting. Audience members couldn't believe their eyes when they saw a pale and unsteady Roosevelt. He was still wearing the bloodied shirt and showed the crowd the bullet-holed pages of his speech. Even in this tragic condition, Roosevelt talked for nearly 90

John Schrank was found insane and placed in the Wisconsin Central State Hospital for the Insane, never to be released. He died in 1943. Mr. Schrank was from New York.

Memorial to the attempted assassination of President Roosevelt

minutes and delivered his entire speech. Once the address was over, the bull moose allowed his companions to take him to the hospital for treatment.

Roosevelt lost the election to Woodrow Wilson but never lost the bullet; it stayed in his chest for the rest of his life.

THEODORE ROOSEVELT ASSASSINATION ATTEMPT

WHAT: Theodore Roosevelt shooting site

WHERE: Hyatt Regency Milwaukee, 333 W Kilbourn Ave., Milwaukee

COST: Free

PRO TIP: In the early 1940s, the Hotel Gilpatrick was torn down, and in the 1970s, the Hyatt Regency was built in its place. The Hyatt has a historical display and a historical monument to the shooting. The collection is located on the hotel's ground floor; just ask at the front desk. It is definitely worth parking for.

GLASS BENDERS

Where can you see art drawn with lights?

Finding Americana by road trips through small towns and along two-lane highways is rewarding. In Wisconsin, it's a given that quirky surprises usually await even on the shortest of day trips. Look in downtown Antigo at Yesterday's Sign Park for a glimpse of neon signs in their heyday. Dean Blazek's private collection of vintage signs brightly lights up the dark sky as a history lesson about the town's businesses from the past.

YESTERDAY'S SIGN PARK

WHAT: Vintage park of neon and vintage signs

WHERE: Corner of 5th Ave. and Clermont St., Antigo

COST: Free

PRO TIP: For the best results, take photos at dusk before the night sky becomes too dark.

Blazek wanted visitors to venture back into town, so he bought the vacant downtown lot where David's Clothier sat. He built the park with vintage neon and porcelain signs representing local businesses that existed from 1930 to 1960—recognizable national brands like Shell gasoline from the filling station, Rexall Drugs that hung at the pharmacy, and a dangling Schlitz beer sign. Local mom-and-pop signs such as Crosley home appliances and radios are also displayed.

Not only is Blazek a passionate sign collector, but he's also a world-renowned neon sign maker. After high school, his dad, a beer rep who also collected neon signs from his brands, suggested Dean learn the neon business. Blazek moved to Milwaukee in 1952 to learn the neon trade from Everbrite Electric Signs, Inc., the largest company of its kind in the Midwest. Three years later, he opened his shop, Northern Advertising, in Antigo. Success followed. The Wisconsin Sign Association recognized his skills and wanted him to teach classes. Thus, the Northern Wisconsin Neon Workshop began

Top: *Neon sign workshop, where all the magic happens. Photo courtesy of Gail Schroepfer.* Inset: *Yesterday's Sign Park in Antigo. Photo courtesy of Antigo/Langlade County Chamber of Commerce*

in 1981. Now, students from around the globe attribute their success to a man who pursued his artistic passion out of high school through glass bending and colors fashioned out of gases. At 89, Dean Blazek still keeps his artistic passion glowing with his love for sketching barns.

Experience America's love affair with neon in the small town of Antigo.

Georges Claude, a French engineer and a neon lighting pioneer, revealed neon for the first time at the Paris Motor Show in 1910.

A ROUND DISC THAT HANGS FROM A STRING

Is there Luck in Yo-Yoing?

Most people think of rural Luck, Wisconsin, as a vacation paradise filled with trees, lakes, and abundant wildlife. However, in 1946, a man named Duncan had a different vision. Thanks to Luck's luck, nearly every adult living there was offered a job.

Don Duncan Sr. entered the yo-yo business in the 1920s and patented the name "yo-yo." He was manufacturing them in Chicago until 1946, when he moved the production operation to Luck, Wisconsin, because of the area's rich supply of maple trees. Hardwood was what the toys were made of at the time. Duncan was also experiencing labor issues in his Chicago plant. In contrast, there was no shortage of workers in rural Luck. So he purchased an old chicken coop with a wood-drying kiln already in place.

The plant blossomed in Luck, and Duncan bought out many of his competitors. By 1962, Duncan Yo-Yo was reaching 90 percent of the yo-yo market. At the peak of the yo-yo craze, Luck was producing 70,000 yo-yos per day and over 20 million per year.

YO-YO CAPITAL OF THE WORLD

WHAT: Yo-Yo Capital of the World Museum

WHERE: Luck, Wisconsin (museum at 301 Main St. S, Luck, inside the public library)

COST: Free

PRO TIP: The museum in Luck has a beautiful display of vintage yo-yos and memorabilia. There are also yo-yos for sale.

Don Duncan Sr. founded the Good Humor mobile frozen treats franchise and a car-meter manufacturing company.

Left: *The Yo-Yo museum is home to many different versions of the toy.*
Right: *Who doesn't remember playing with a Yo-Yo? Some of us still do.*

In 1965, due to rising production costs, dropping sales, shrinking market share, and the changing toy landscape, the yo-yo factory in Luck was shut down. However, a plastics company, Flambeau Plastics, purchased the trademarked Duncan brand name and has continued to make the yo-yos ever since.

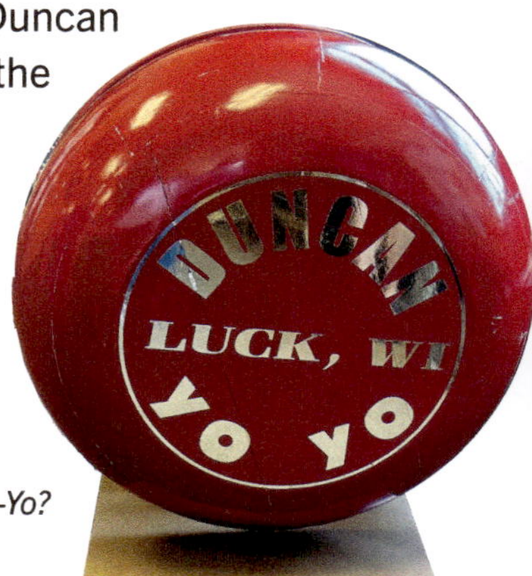

Is it the world's biggest Yo-Yo?

THE BATTLE IS STILL RAGING IN WISCONSIN

Butter or oleomargarine? The choice is not yours!

In the early 1870s, the French product oleomargarine made its way to the kitchens of Wisconsin. Oleomargarine was cheaper than butter, kept longer, and was more consistent in quality than local butter. This started the war that still rages today.

The Wisconsin Dairymen's Association (WDA) started in 1872 with the top priority of stopping the spread of oleomargarine in the state. To do this, they improved the quality of the butter and worked with politicians to fight off the new competitor. In 1881, the first antimargarine law was passed, which put specific labeling on packaging to avoid confusion between the two. Five years later, the legislators enacted more stringent regulations, including taxes and more defined packaging. Fans of butter didn't want oleomargarine sold, and fans of the inexpensive oleomargarine were angered by the high tax and lack of availability of their product.

By 1950, oleomargarine was still being taxed at 15 cents per pound, significant at a time when the minimum wage was 75 cents an hour. This tax created a new problem: the smuggling of oleo across borders by Wisconsinites. It was estimated that a ton of margarine came across Wisconsin's southern border every week.

Finally, on April 5, 1967, voices of oleo supporters were heard, and the state assembly voted to allow the sale of

---

All of the butter for brands across the country is made at a few plants. The plants use different recipes and labels for a variety of brands.

Butter versus margarine, which would you choose?

oleomargarine. So, on July 1, 1967, for the first time in 72 years, colored oleomargarine was legal in Wisconsin. But not in restaurants. Only butter could be served in restaurants unless a patron specifically ordered oleomargarine. This law was tested in 2004, when a patron ordered a baked potato from the Ponderosa Steakhouse in Menomonee Falls. The potato arrived smothered in margarine. The patron asked for butter, and the server stated they didn't have any. The patron filed a complaint with the local health and human services department, and the restaurant was cited. The butter battle rages on.

THE BUTTER BATTLE

WHAT: Wisconsin butter battle

WHERE: Wisconsin

COST: Depends on which side you are on: butter or margarine.

PRO TIP: There is a code on every package of butter that indicates the plant number and state. For example, in the code 55-1457, 55 is the state, and 1457 is the plant. To find out where your butter is from, take your butter's code to mydatcp.wi.gov.

FRIDAY MORNING FISH FRY

Where can you buy fish and shrimp at a bakery?

On Friday mornings, customers line up inside Oliver's Bakery to take part in an iconic Wisconsin institution: the Friday fish fry. In the midst of magnificently crafted doughnuts and pastries, hot, deep-fried fish and shrimp appear each Friday morning until they sell out. A majority of the crispy golden brown battered seafood is preordered by phone. Walk-in customers might be lucky if they arrive early enough. No one really knows when the bakery began offering Fish Fry Friday. The bakery started in 1949, but owner Anne Benson has helped carry on the tradition since she started working there in 1978.

Besides a delicious Friday meal, Oliver's Bakery creates scrumptious bakery goods every day except for Sunday: 20 Kringle flavors, muffins, danishes, specialty cookies, and an exceptional variety of extra-large doughnuts. Doughnuts barely hold their fillings, and the weight from buttercream frosting collapses the tops of the Cyclops. A Cyclops is a raised doughnut hand-dipped in chocolate with a squirt of buttercream in the middle. When Fat Tuesday rolls around, a crew and staff of volunteers pack the bakery for paczki production. Overnight, the crew makes and then fills about 3,000 of these Polish filled doughnuts until they almost burst. Oliver's usually has six to nine flavors to choose from, but they may only have a few hundred available for walk-ins, so call ahead of time with an order.

Visiting the 1949 building with its classic Americana neon sign is like stepping back in time. Ask owner Anne Benson about the bakery's history.

Left: *This neon sign is a great way to welcome the day.* Right: *At 9 a.m. on a Friday, do you choose a piece of fish or a danish? Oliver's Bakery serves both.*

OLIVER'S BAKERY

WHAT: Traditional bakery that cooks fish and shrimp on Friday mornings

WHERE: 3526 Roosevelt Rd., Kenosha

COST: Deep fried cod is $14 per pound, shrimp is $18 per pound.

PRO TIP: Order a cake ahead of time.

With a bakery full of exceptional treats, the best item may be its cakes. Oliver's is an old-fashioned bakery, the kind that is quickly disappearing. All bakery items, including cakes, are made from scratch. The bakery's extraordinary buttercream frosting is made in-house. Along with traditional cakes, wedding and party cakes are a specialty. Some are even quirky—for instance, a lifelike plate of spaghetti and meatballs, a grilled cheese sandwich cut in half with an order of fries, and a cake for National Pencil Day.

A TV REPAIR SHOP WITH A TWIST

Can a TV repair shop help an empty stomach?

We had heard of this place but had no idea what we were about to find when we arrived. We walked in the front door to a small room with groceries and a pinball machine. At the counter, a clerk asked if we had a repair we were dropping off or picking up. We said we were there for the burgers. The clerk said we must have been in the wrong place, which went back and forth for a few minutes. Eventually, she asked if we were thirsty, and this is when we finally caught on. There is a password needed to enter. Once we were able to persuade the clerk for the password, a pop machine on the wall opened up, revealing the secret passage that led to the hidden restaurant.

The restaurant inside Don's TV and Repair is like a blast from the past, with low lighting, dark corner booths, and '80s and '90s pop culture décor all around. A restored 1950s vintage jukebox plays upbeat music. Vintage TVs and VCRs are playing '80s movies

DON'S TV AND REPAIR

WHAT: A speakeasy retro restaurant

WHERE: 1100 S 1st St., Milwaukee, donsmke.com/tvrepair

COST: Menu prices

PRO TIP: Due to the small capacity, booking your "service appointment" online is recommended. Enter through Don's Grocery & Liquor door. Ask the clerk for an "ice-cold 7 Up."

Don's Grocery & Liquor has all the essentials if you are not hungry but need toilet paper or a pack of Twinkies.

Left: *If you know the password, you can pass through the vintage 7UP pop machine door.* Right: *Don's TV & Repair, Milwaukee.*

in every corner. Lots of vintage video game consoles and electronic advertising memorabilia adorn the walls. It's like walking into a basement rec room all over again.

The restaurant is known for burgers, boozy shakes, and Fruity-Pebble pancakes. Don's also serves your favorite cocktails with a twist. On Thursday nights there are 10-cent martinis, and on Wednesdays burgers are 99 cents with the purchase of a drink.

TURKEYS IN THE BASEMENT

Where can you bowl in America's oldest sanctioned bowling alley?

Two illuminated legs and shoes dangle between the pins in the nation's oldest sanctioned bowling alley's only two lanes. After a ball crashes through pins, energetic pinsetters—many of them kids, grandkids, and family friends—jump up to manually reload pins and drop the ball onto the vintage wood return track. According to Catherine and Tom Haefkey, fifth-generation owners, the original lanes are built from cherry and pine wood.

Located in the basement of the Holler House in a Milwaukee Polish south-side neighborhood, the bar and bowling alley have been operating since 1908. In 1910, the bowling alley was sanctioned and continues to pass yearly certifications.

Professional bowlers and people in the spotlight seek out the Holler House to bowl a few frames when in Milwaukee. Jack White from the White Stripes, a passionate bowler, reserved the lanes when he was in town for a concert. Joe Walsh from the Eagles also bowled here. Although many notable people consider bowling at the Holler House a feather in their cap, the bar's popularity can be attributed to Catherine's mom, Marcy, a lady full of zest and liked by everyone.

Marcy, a jokester with a quick wit and a legendary storyteller, initiated the bar's newcomer bra tradition. During the women's liberation movement, several couples visited the bar together. The men were ready to leave, but the women were not. After

---

From manually reloading pins to keeping score on paper attached to the wall, bowling here is an old-fashioned experience.

Left: *The oldest sanctioned bowling alley in the nation.* Right: *Pinsetters still set the pins by hand at Milwaukee's Holler House.*

each round of drinks, the men became more agitated and insisted that they leave. Marcy told the women to follow her into the kitchen, where she devised a plan. The tradition began when the women left the kitchen wearing less than they walked in with, then flung their bras so that they hung from the ceiling.

HOLLER HOUSE

WHAT: The oldest sanctioned bowling alley in the nation

WHERE: 2042 W Lincoln Ave., Milwaukee

COST: $5 a game per bowler, plus a tip for pinsetter. Minimum of $50 to reserve per hour.

PRO TIP: Bring cash—no other form of payment is accepted.

OTIS REDDING'S LAST FLIGHT

What did Lake Monona witness?

The weather forecast was foggy and cold, but that didn't stop a determined performer who wanted to make his fans happy. Otis Redding was in Cleveland, Ohio, on the morning of December 10, 1967, when he boarded his private twin-engine Beechcraft H18 plane to fly to Madison, Wisconsin, for an evening concert at the Factory on Gorham Street.

By this time, Otis Redding was a massive European star and didn't have to drive from gig to gig. His career was taking off in the United States, and so was he. He had his own airplane and pilot to take him from place to place.

On that fateful December afternoon at around 3:30, Otis Redding's plane crashed into Lake Monona with Otis and his band, a total of eight passengers, aboard. The airplane was above Squaw Bay when it was given permission to land, and after traveling another mile it crashed into the lake. The FAA stated there was no distress call or indication of trouble with the approach, and contact was lost at 3:25. The plane went down about a half mile from the 4600 block of Tonyawatha Trail in Monona Village. There was one survivor, a band member.

OTIS REDDING PLANE CRASH

WHAT: Plaque memorializing the plane crash that killed Otis Redding

WHERE: On the rooftop garden of Monona Terrace Convention Center, 1 John Nolen Dr., Madison

COST: Free

PRO TIP: The rooftop garden of Monona Terrace is open daily from 8 a.m. to 10 p.m. Parking is available.

Monona Terrace is home to the Otis Redding Memorial.

As evening approached, the fans waiting outside the Factory were restless and had not heard the news. Otis Redding would not show up for his scheduled concert. Instead, the fans would only hear the opening act, ironically named The Grim Reapers. After the tragedy, The Grim Reapers changed their name to Cheap Trick.

Otis Redding died just three days after recording "(Sittin' On) the Dock of the Bay," which became the first posthumous number one single in US chart history.

PANCAKES FROM OUT OF THIS WORLD

What would Simon say?

Wisconsin has a long history of UFO sightings and experiences. Many are familiar, but many are not.

According to Eagle River plumber and farmer Joe Simonton, he was having breakfast on April 18, 1961, when a spaceship landed in his yard. He decided to investigate. When he approached the craft, the door opened, and he could see figures inside. Simonton described the aliens as very small with dark hair, dark skin, and dark eyes. One had a metal jug, and Simonton somehow discerned that the figures needed water, so he filled up their jug for them. When he returned to the craft with the water, one of the aliens was cooking what looked like pancakes on a flameless appliance. The visitors gave Joe some of the pancakes, saluted him, and flew away the way they had arrived. Once the craft left, Joe ate one of the pancakes and said it tasted like cardboard.

In addition to Joe's experience with flying objects, the Eagle River area suffered a vast power failure the following month, and the telephone lines went down. A fighter jet crashed 60

JOE SIMONTON'S UFO

WHAT: Story of Joe Simonton's UFO encounter

WHERE: A farm outside Eagle River

COST: Free

PRO TIP: The case of Joe Simonton's UFO still remains unexplained by the Air Force.

The pancakes were collected by the US Air Force and tested by the FDA, and the ingredients were found to be of earthly origin.

Here's the "pancake from outer space" that caused nationwide publicity for Eagle River beginning Saturday of last week—and still continuing. It is held by Joe Simonton, 54, of Eagle River, who alleges it was given to him by three men who landed in his yard in a flying saucer. The novel and incredible story

United Press International, and leading television stations and metropolitan newspapers. One of the pancakes has been sent by Judge Frank W. Carter to Donald E. Keyhoe, director of the National Investigating Committee on Aerial Phenomena, Washington, D. C. Keyhoe is having the pancake analyzed.—NEWS-REVIEW photo

Joe with his out of this world pancake. Photo courtesy of Vilas County News-Review

miles from Eagle River, and later in May, another plane crashed near the area. This area has reported many UFO sightings from 1959 to 1963. Coincidence?

Because there were other reports of UFO sightings in the area of Simonton's farm, the United States Air Force investigated the story, and it is still listed in their files as "unexplained."

I'VE GOT ALL MY SISTERS WITH ME

Can you easily walk from Paris to China?

Enacted on September 11, 1956, by President Dwight D. Eisenhower, the sister city program promotes peace through mutual respect, understanding, and cooperation, one community at a time. Eisenhower felt that people from different cultures could understand, appreciate, and celebrate differences while building partnerships that would reduce the chance of new world conflicts. La Crosse is a good representation of this. They have partnered with seven different international cities: Luoyang, China (1997); Friedberg, Germany (2002); Dubna, Russia (1990); Forde, Norway (2005); Epinal, France (1986); Bantry, Ireland (2005); and Kumbo, Cameroon (2013).

The Riverside International Friendship Gardens honor and pay tribute to La Crosse sister cities. Walk along the small boardwalk and stroll through the seven distinctive gardens. The Chinese garden features a dragon gate, koi pond, and plants native to China. The German garden features a large golden sculpture of a pocket watch. The Russian garden has a round domed structure that replicates one on the Volga River. The Norwegian garden has a sod-roofed structure and seven trolls.

Chinese entry into the International Friendship Park

Left: *Eiffel Tower in the French section of La Crosse's International Friendship Park.*
Right: *Tribute to the Russian sister city*

A miniature Le Pinau statue is highlighted in the French garden, along with an Eiffel Tower replica. The lush, green garden with the mill wheel is representative of Ireland. Finally, Cameroon's garden has tropical plants and red ground cover, representing the red soil in Cameroon.

RIVERSIDE INTERNATIONAL FRIENDSHIP GARDENS

WHAT: International Friendship Gardens representing sister cities of La Crosse

WHERE: 345–405 E Veterans Memorial Dr., La Crosse

COST: Free, donation box

PRO TIP: The park is open daily from 6 a.m. to 11 p.m. It is wheelchair accessible, and parking is adjacent to the gardens. Leashed dogs are welcome.

Sister Cities International is open to cities, countries, and states of all sizes. Currently, there are over 2,000 partners in more than 140 countries.

WINTER LAYUP

Where do the Lakers recuperate in winter?

Seeing massive ships close-up on the Great Lakes takes planning and a lot of luck. Although these imposing ships—some over 1,000 feet long—constantly haul loads of taconite, coal, grains, limestone, and other products across the lakes, the best time to see them is when they are entering or leaving ports. Elated onlookers feel like children, no matter how many times a "Laker" glides a few feet away. On the Great Lakes, ship spotting is like a sport. Passionate fans hold their favorites close to their hearts. Some cry when they see them, and others proudly boast by sharing their photos on social media. Either way, fervent ship spotters consider it a feather in their hat when they stand beside a 1,000-footer as it passes nearby.

However, each year has a quiet season, winter layup, when the ice on the Great Lakes becomes too thick to navigate. Shipping halts for about 10 weeks, depending on the weather. At season's end, each freighter company sends its ships to different ports across the Great Lakes for repairs and routine maintenance. Crews normally take time off during this period. Some spend time with their families, while others work at ports doing maintenance and repairs.

Fincantieri Bay Shipbuilding, at Sturgeon Bay, one of the largest shipbuilding companies in America, accommodates a large fleet of ships during winter hiatus from different companies. The shipyard offers an excellent place to see an abundance of ships close up. Three of the best places to ship-spot are across Sturgeon Bay at Bullhead Point, driving

---

A sailor's life is often demanding, requiring a round-the-clock commitment. Many work a 60/30 schedule, spending 60 days on board followed by a break of 30 days.

Sturgeon Bay is a perfect way to see a large number of Great Lake freighters up close and in one place. Photo courtesy of Tim Manus Photography

past the shipyard on North 3rd Avenue, and at Sunset Park off of Florida Street. To experience how massive these ships are, drive down Florida Street, which runs parallel to a dock of considerable length.

SEE GREAT LAKES FREIGHTERS CLOSE-UP

WHAT: Viewing ships when the Great Lakes are frozen

WHERE: Sturgeon Bay

COST: Free

PRO TIP: Visit the Door County Maritime Museum. Tour a restored tugboat and see a working lighthouse.

AMERICA'S FIRST DAIRY SCHOOL

How has Babcock Dairy shaped ice cream history?

Ice cream lovers worldwide are forever indebted to a University of Wisconsin–Madison dairy scientist's invention. Soon after chemist Stephen Babcock arrived on campus in 1890, he developed an easy test to determine the butterfat content of milk. The method, later called the Babcock butterfat test, allowed creameries to select the best milk for their products, thus significantly improving the state's dairy products and boosting Wisconsin's reputation as a world leader in quality dairy products, including ice cream.

UW–Madison's Babcock Dairy Store serves premium flavors of Babcock Dairy ice cream made with the freshest milk from the university's dairy herd down the street. The UW dairy plant uses premium ingredients like pure vanilla and real sugar with the same recipes since 1951. Each year, new flavors appear alongside established favorites. Some of the most popular flavors are Orange Custard Chocolate Chip, Berry Alvarez, Union Utopia, Blue Moon, and Chocolate Peanut Butter. Unusual flavors from the past include Cantaloupe, Sunflower Pecan Butterscotch Swirl, Licorice Chip, Peach Melba, and Monk's Madness—brandy flavored with hazelnuts. Occasionally, flavors don't sell as well as hoped. Peanut Butter and Jelly, Sunflower Seed, and Christmas Surprise are examples.

BABCOCK DAIRY STORE

WHAT: Ice cream made at University of Wisconsin–Madison

WHERE: 1605 Linden Dr., Madison

COST: $4.59 small, $6.49 large, either in a dish or cake cone

PRO TIP: To avoid long lines, visit in January and February, the slowest-selling months.

Get a special Wisconsin treat from Babcock Dairy Store

Ice cream makes memories. Many have been made on the other side of Lake Monona at the Monona Bait and Ice Cream Shop, where families have been lining up for Babcock Dairy ice cream seemingly forever. Grandparents remember eating a cone in front of the shop, or at Schluter Beach, across the street, as kids. Whether arriving by car, by the bike path, or by boat, getting an old-fashioned hand-dipped cone at the bait shop seems like stepping back in time.

Butterfat amount helps determine ice cream quality. Standard grade has around 10 percent butterfat, which is the government minimum. Premium grade contains between 12 and 14 percent, and super premium can contain up to 17 percent.

A BUSINESSMAN'S RETREAT

Where do mobsters go to escape the heat?

There was a time when the Northwoods of Wisconsin attracted more than just run-of-the-mill tourists. During the 1920s, Chicago mobsters started coming to the Northwoods to escape the heat being put on them in the city. The Northwoods was an easy place to hide but still allowed the gangsters to conduct their business.

Al Capone was one of these so-called businessmen. From 1924 to 1931, Al Capone was one of Chicago's most notorious organized crime bosses. He was involved with bootlegging, racketeering, gambling, and also murder. He was ruthless and relied on bribes, violence, and intimidation to accomplish his goals during the Prohibition era.

Capone built his 407-acre retreat, or hideout as it was called, north of Couderay in Sawyer County to escape the city for rest and relaxation. The complex is set back off the road with large fieldstone pillar gates. Down a long driveway hidden in a tall forest sits a large, stone, two-story main house with 18-inch-thick walls. The property also had a bunkhouse used by Capone's henchmen, an eight-car garage, and a machine-gun lookout tower—everything Al needed for a restful retreat up north.

The hideout had frontage on the 37-acre Pike Lake. The lake proved helpful for the mobster in the transport of liquor during prohibition. Capone's gang would transport booze from

---

Ralph Capone, Al's brother, owned and operated the Rex Hotel and Billy's Bar in Mercer until the 1970s, when he died.

A view above Al Capone's hideout. Photo courtesy of Tim Manus Photography

Canada in floatplanes to his private retreat and then truck the liquor to Chicago.

The property is currently unused, with No Trespassing signs surrounding it.

THE HIDEOUT

WHAT: Al Capone's Northwoods hideout complex

WHERE: 12101 County Rd. CC, Couderay

COST: Free

PRO TIP: Capone was eventually convicted of income tax evasion and spent much of his sentence at the infamous Alcatraz prison in San Francisco. He died in 1947 at the age of 48.

SPOONER FISH HATCHERY

Why would someone cast 10,000 times to catch a fish?

Wisconsin's state fish, the musky, short for muskellunge, is an enormous creature with a big attitude. The elusive but ferocious fish tempts anglers to keep casting in hopes of landing a trophy fish. It's often referred to as "the fish of 10,000 casts," and anglers try to earn bragging rights by reeling in the torpedo-shaped fish with a huge head and a mouth full of teeth that can grow up to one inch. Wisconsin's top areas to try catching a musky are Hayward, Vilas County, and Green Bay. The biggest musky on record—69 pounds and 11 ounces—was caught near Hayward in the Chippewa Flowage.

Wisconsin holds more musky world records than anywhere else, and you can see where these beastly fish are reared at the world's largest musky fish hatchery in Spooner. The hatchery provides more than half of the state's musky and walleye by collecting over 100 million fresh eggs yearly from the wild. After eggs are incubated inside the facility, biologists and DNR employees release the fingerlings into 40 one-acre and 6 half-acre ponds next to the facility. On average, the hatchery produces 35,000 to 60,000 large muskies and 200,000 to 2.5 million walleyes yearly. Additionally, about 21 million white suckers are raised each year for food.

GOVERNOR TOMMY G. THOMPSON STATE FISH HATCHERY

WHAT: The world's largest musky fish hatchery

WHERE: 951 W Maple St., Spooner

COST: Free

PRO TIP: The best time to see incubation is May.

Top: *All things fish are displayed at the Spooner Fish Hatchery.* Inset: *An abundance of fish eggs.*

Tour the visitors center year-round, Monday through Friday from 8 a.m. to 3 p.m. to learn about incubators, fish anatomy, water ecology, and how a fish hatchery works. You can even ask for fishing advice. Inside are exhibits, artifacts, and vintage fishing-lure collections. One collection belongs to a DNR supervisor. After touring, try fishing in the adjacent Veterans Memorial Waterfront Park. The best fishing is at the dam. However, a river and lake offer excellent angling too.

Ruth King, a DNR biologist since 1986, painted the 24-foot mural inside the visitors center. The mural represents a typical Wisconsin lake scene above and below the water.

FROM SPROCKETS TO ROCKETS

Bikes, airplanes, astronauts, and moon rocks: what's the connection?

There is a museum in Sparta that traces the line from bicycles to space exploration. The Wright brothers used bicycle parts from their bike shop to create the first flying machine. Planes then needed pilots, and some of those pilots went on to become astronauts. Sparta, the "Bicycling Capital of America," needed a bicycle museum. Sparta was also home to Donald "Deke" Slayton, a Mercury astronaut. So why not combine the two into one museum?

The museum is home to many pieces of Astronaut Slayton's memorabilia, including his 1959 never-used spacesuit and plaster molds of his hands, which reveal he didn't have a left ring finger; it was severed in a farm accident as a child. Hanging from the ceiling of the small museum is the cherry-red race plane that Slayton flew after retirement from NASA.

A unique find at the museum is the only moon rock in Wisconsin. The rock was given to Deke Slayton's widow as part of the Ambassador of Exploration Award. His widow chose the museum to display the moon rock, which can be seen by all visitors.

The museum captures over 200 years of the history of bicycling as well. On display are more than 80 bicycles from throughout history up to the modern day. One of the bikes is an ice bike. Instead of a front wheel, it has an ice skating blade,

---

The museum complex is part of Sparta's historic four corners. On each corner of the intersection is a historic building: the museum complex, courthouse, library, and post office.

Follow the progression of bicycles through the years.

and the back wheel is spiked so it can be ridden on frozen lakes. Unfortunately, the bike was only available briefly because it was deemed far too dangerous.

DEKE SLAYTON MEMORIAL SPACE & BICYCLE MUSEUM

WHAT: A museum dedicated to rockets and sprockets

WHERE: 200 W Main St., Sparta

COST: $5

PRO TIP: The museum hosts a space camp during the summer for kids in third through eighth grades. During the weeklong camps, kids talk with pilots, learn about airplanes, visit a planetarium, and participate in the building of rockets.

WORKING NINE TO THREE ON THE ROOF

Why are there goats on the roof of this restaurant?

In 1949, Al Johnson started a little Scandinavian restaurant where he hoped his friends and neighbors would gather. Over the years, he continued to grow and remodel the restaurant. Finally, in 1973, he found the final piece to the puzzle while on a trip to Scandinavia with his wife. The couple purchased a Norwegian log façade for the restaurant. The façade was built in Norway, taken apart, numbered, and shipped to Sister Bay. Once the façade was rebuilt, a sod roof was added to the restaurant. Eventually, goats were also introduced to the roof, just like on the sod roofs in Scandinavia.

Every morning from May through mid-October, the goats make their short office commute. Once there, they walk the ramp to the top of the restaurant and start their day eating grass, entertaining the tourists, but most of all, posing for photos. There are usually about 8 to 10 goats peering down from the roof as you enter the restaurant.

At the beginning of the season, the annual Roofing of the Goats Parade and Festival is held. The parade takes the goats down Main Street and culminates with the placement of the

AL JOHNSON'S SWEDISH RESTAURANT & BUTIK

WHAT: A restaurant with goats on the roof

WHERE: 10698 N Bay Shore Dr., Sister Bay

COST: Free to see goats, menu prices for food

PRO TIP: Can't make it to the restaurant? Check out the Goat Cam. Two cameras are mounted on top of the restaurant that catch 95 percent of the sod, so as long as the goats are working, you should be able to catch a glimpse.

One of Al Johnson's goats posing for photos. Photo courtesy of Jon Jarosh/ Destination Door County

first goats of the season on the restaurant's sod roof. After the parade, the Goat Fest gets started. The fest includes live music, games, and a Swedish pancake–eating contest.

The goats arrive on the roof at about 9 a.m. and stay until 3 p.m. The goats, divas that they are, are weather dependent, and if it is cold, windy, or raining heavily, you won't see them on the roof.

A Door County restaurant with goats working on the roof. Photo courtesy of Jon Jarosh/Destination Door County

BOXING WILDLIFE

Where can you see Northwoods wildlife satirizing human behavior?

Inside the Moccasin Bar, a sprightly poker game between two anglers is in full swing. On one side of the table Royal Flush Joe, a bear cub smoking a corn-cob pipe with his shotgun by his side, holds his cards with one paw while the other secretly slips a carrot to a white rabbit dressed to the nines. Standing behind the cub on her back feet and in pearls, she holds an ace of hearts in her extended front foot in exchange for the carrot. On the other side, Full House Pete, a badger wearing a red fishing hat with lures attached, lays cash on the table with his right paw while his left paw holds his cards. Behind Pete, an otter pours another bottle of beer into a glass. In this particular wildlife exhibit, characters have adult beverage bottles throughout the sportsmen's lodge scene.

Wildlife dioramas like this line the walls throughout the bar, along with some really big fish. You'll see a boxing match where a beaver holds a fox's arm in the air proclaiming him the winner over a raccoon. Skunk managers stand behind each boxer, holding towels. In the Northwoods Kangaroo Court, Judge Wolf presides over Squealer Muskrat and Violator Badger. In Seven Come 'Leven, four chipmunks sing "Sweet Adeline" with fishing squirrels around them. These are just a few of the quirky wildlife exhibits intertwined with huge, record-breaking fish.

Many giant-sized muskies hang all through the bar in Hayward, the "Muskie Capital of the World," including Cal Johnson's

---

The bar has been around since the 1880s. According to locals, the bizarre wildlife was bought from taxidermists in the 1930s and has been in the bar ever since.

Top left: *Moccasin Bar, Hayward.* Above left: *The Moccasin Bar is full of quirky stuffed wildlife.* Top right: *Stuffed wildlife playing poker in Moccasin Bar.* Above right: *World's Largest Record Muskellunge caught by Cal Johnson in 1949*

67-pound, 8-ounce, 59.5-inch-long world-record catch from the summer of 1949. Three months later, the record was broken again, by three ounces, at the nearby Chippewa Flowage, then again in 1957 in upstate New York.

MOCCASIN BAR

WHAT: Classic Northwoods bar filled with quirky wildlife dioramas

WHERE: 15820 US Hwy. 63, Hayward

COST: Free

PRO TIP: Visit the Freshwater Fishing Hall of Fame, also in Hayward

EVEN FUTURE PRESIDENTS NEED TO USE THE FACILITIES

Why is this urinal a tourist attraction?

On March 18, 1960, during the Democratic presidential primary campaign, then-Senator John F. Kennedy gave a campaign speech on Walnut Street in downtown Spooner. The senator was canvassing the northwest section of Wisconsin in hopes of winning the Democratic primary. Landing in Eau Claire, he started the five-day hand-shaking trip. Unfortunately, he had a hard road ahead. His primary opponent was Minnesota's Hubert Humphrey, who was well-liked in this part of the state. Nevertheless, Kennedy made campaign stops in every small town, club, school, and main street that would have him. In Ladysmith, Kennedy stopped to talk to a group of nuns standing alongside the road and even visited their convent. It was a long and busy five days with many unplanned stops.

PRESIDENTIAL URINAL

WHAT: Urinal that John F. Kennedy used

WHERE: Big Dick's Buckhorn Inn, 105 Walnut St., Spooner

COST: Free, urinal in back

PRO TIP: Check out the vast collection of taxidermied fish and wildlife throughout the bar, including a two-headed calf.

The bar has lots of vintage brewery signs and memorabilia and even has a wood and glass back bar installed by the Leinenkugel brewery in the 1930s.

Top: *Big Dick's Buckhorn Inn in downtown Spooner.* Inset: *This restroom was visited by John F. Kennedy on a campaign stop in Spooner.*

Eventually, the road led to Spooner, where Kennedy gave a speech in the middle of the street in front of Buckhorn Inn. When he finished with the address, he went into the bar, and someone bought him a beer. Kennedy didn't finish the beer, but he did have to use the restroom. A clever proprietor capitalized on this and made a plaque memorializing the occurrence. "John F. Kennedy used these facilities March 18, 1960."

The plaque and urinal are still present, along with many other quirky bar decorations.

ENTER THIS WILD WOOD AND VIEW THE HAUNTS OF NATURE

A peaceful walk or a haunted adventure?

A gem of the south side of Milwaukee, Grant Park is a beautiful forest park located along the shores of Lake Michigan. Inside the park is the Seven Bridges Trail. The trail winds through an almost enchanted forest with towering trees, rolling mounds, and meandering streams. Along the trail are bridges and stairways built over 100 years ago. The trail and park make you feel like you are part of a fairy tale.

You begin the trail by crossing under a covered bridge with "Enter this wild wood and view the haunts of nature" inscribed overhead. It's a tranquil and peaceful walk during the day, when the trail is full of families and strollers, but when moonlight appears, the park supposedly takes on a frightening alter ego. Then you may spot a misty apparition floating near you or hear the terrified screams from deep in the empty woods. There are even reports of footsteps and heavy breathing coming from behind, only to pass suddenly, leaving a frightening feeling in their wake. Those claiming to have experienced the lore are numerous and convincing.

SEVEN BRIDGES TRAIL IN GRANT PARK

WHAT: Haunted trail

WHERE: 100 Hawthorne Ave., Milwaukee

COST: Free

PRO TIP: Grant Park has beautiful beach access, numerous picnic spots with tables, and a disc golf course.

Seven Bridges Trail was constructed by a WPA crew during the Great Depression.

A relaxing walk in the daylight, but it can be rattling after dark.

Rumors have haunted this park for years. The best way to find out the truth is to investigate it yourself. Are you ready to walk the Seven Bridges Trail by moonlight? Keep in mind that the park closes at 10 p.m.

HEARTY APPETITE

What do lumberjacks like to eat?

Paul Bunyan's legend lives on in Wisconsin Dells. Bunyan, a lumberjack folk hero and legend since the mid-1800s, cleared entire forests with a single swing of the axe and, along with his companion, Babe the Blue Ox, scooped out the Great Lakes to supply water for fellow lumberjacks. At Paul Bunyan's Cook Shanty in Wisconsin Dells, the doughnuts have risen to the same stature as the fabled lumberjack. Although people visit the logging camp–themed restaurant for a Northwoods experience, most leave with fond memories of its homemade pastry.

Each day the baker arrives at 5 a.m. to start making doughnut batter. By 7 a.m., before hungry guests walk in the door, staff stock the pastry counter with different varieties, including chocolate covered, plain, some with sprinkles, elephant ears, and even cookies. But the buttermilk sugar-coated doughnuts are a big deal. They sell thousands of these hot, freshly made doughnuts daily, with staff constantly restocking up front. Many guests buy a pack of 6 or 12 on the way out the door, but anyone can walk in and pick them up at the gift shop counter.

Doughnuts connect us to Northwoods lumberjack life. Between the late 1800s and early 1900s, logging camp cooks made doughnuts daily with a hearty breakfast. Some would

All-you-can-eat lumberjack breakfast at Paul Bunyan's Cook Shanty.

argue that they were the best part of the meal. Like customers at the restaurant, lumberjacks were served family-style with platters of food on tables. Paul Bunyan's Cook Shanty resembles an 1890s Northwoods logging camp. Antiques and artifacts on brown log walls surround long wooden tables and benches. Metal plates, bowls, mugs, and utensils sit on top of red-and-white checkered tablecloths. People make memories in the Northwoods. Some of those memories include 1890s logging camp–style doughnuts.

PAUL BUNYAN'S COOK SHANTY

WHAT: 1890s lumberjack-style restaurant

WHERE: 411 State Hwy. 13, Wisconsin Dells

COST: Free to visit the gift shop

PRO TIP: Order doughnuts on the website for pickup or shipping.

The packed gift shop is one of the largest in Wisconsin Dells. More Northwoods-themed gifts can be found downtown in DooHickey's, owned by the same family that owns the shanty.

CLANG, CLANG, CLANG

Where can you feel like you're in San Francisco?

Although riders can't hang off a moving streetcar like in the old television commercials about a rice side dish in San Francisco, they can have a similar experience in Kenosha. Bright, art deco–painted electric streetcars move around a two-mile loop with a clang, clang, clang ringing out from the bell.

See the North Pier Lighthouse, a beach, Harbor Park, and Southport Marina along the scenic Lake Michigan shoreline and downtown route. If you prefer, you can get off the streetcar and walk along the waterfront to see sculptures, fountains, and gardens or visit museums. Downtown offers restaurants, shopping, parks, and a farmers market on Saturday. Streetcars have wheelchair-accessible lifts.

Electric streetcar use in Kenosha peaked in the early 1900s, then died off as cheaper modes of transportation became available. Fortunately, the vintage mode of transportation returned to Kenosha in June of 2000. The fleet contains seven restored authentic 1948 and 1951 President's Conference Committee (PCC) cars. Six of these cars were used in Toronto from 1951 to 1995, while the seventh was used in Philadelphia from 1948 to 1993.

Each vehicle's paint schemes and lettering from the 1940s and 1950s characterize a city that used PCC streetcars: orange represents Johnstown, Pennsylvania; maroon and cream depict Toronto; Chicago is mostly green with some cream and an orange stripe; and yellow and green represent Cincinnati, though some might mistake it for the colors of the

---

Streetcar technician Joe Lamothe wanted this job since he was a kid. Now, he oversees the program, and his passion overflows in conversations.

Left: *A ride is like a step back in time.* Right: *One of Kenosha's electric streetcars.* Inset: *Kenosha has a fleet of seven restored streetcars.*

STREETCARS IN KENOSHA

WHAT: Historic streetcar rides to see downtown attractions and the harbor

WHERE: Downtown Kenosha

COST: $3.50 all-day pass; $1.00 for ages 13 and up; $0.50 for ages 5 to 12; and ages four and under are free

PRO TIP: Use exact change or a bus pass since change is not provided.

Packers. Red and cream stood out to riders in Pittsburgh, while green and cream greeted customers in San Francisco. Finally, in Philadelphia, red, white, and blue carried passengers to their destinations. Picking a favorite from so many fun, colorful designs becomes difficult.

A NIGHT OF FLAMES

Was it a cow like in Chicago?

On the night of October 8, 1871, fires were breaking out all over the upper Midwest. It had been an arid year, and all the kindling needed was a spark. According to legend, Mrs. O'Leary's cow tipped over a lantern in Chicago and started the most famous of the fires, the Great Chicago Fire. Train workers were clearing the tracks in Peshtigo, which ignited America's deadliest wildfire.

Peshtigo was a tinderbox waiting to ignite. Every structure in town was made of wood, and even the streets were covered in wood chips. The Peshtigo fire moved as swiftly as a tornado, with 200-foot flames. The explosive speed of the flames consumed all available oxygen. With temperatures reaching 2,000 degrees, some trying to flee burst into flames. Many sought refuge in the Peshtigo River, while some went to basements. Building after building ignited so quickly that occupants couldn't get out. The entire town was ablaze within an hour. More than 800 residents

THE GREAT PESHTIGO FIRE

WHAT: Peshtigo Fire Museum

WHERE: 400 Oconto Ave., Peshtigo

COST: Free

PRO TIP: There have been rumors that the Chicago and Peshtigo fires were caused by fragments of a comet smashing into the earth.

The Great Chicago Fire killed some 300 people, destroyed more than 17,000 wooden structures, and far overshadowed the Peshtigo Fire. However, the loss of life was far more significant in Peshtigo.

Left: *The Great Peshtigo Fire Museum.* Right: *A memorial to the Great Peshtigo Fire in 1871.*

were killed by the flames. Those who did make it through the horrific event found an apocalyptic scene the following day.

The fire scorched 16 towns and 1.5 million acres. Then, it jumped across Green Bay and burned Door County, leaving 128 dead. Over 2,400 people were killed in the area, making the Peshtigo Fire America's deadliest wildfire.

The Peshtigo Fire Museum has exhibits and artifacts from the fire and a cemetery memorializing those who perished.

A SCAVENGER HUNT WITHIN THE STATE CAPITOL

What is hidden in plain sight around the inside of the Wisconsin State Capitol?

The focal point of Madison's isthmus, the Wisconsin State Capitol, is an impressive piece of architecture. Built with a granite dome just three feet shy of the height of the dome of the United States Capitol, the Wisconsin State Capitol is 284 feet, 5 inches tall. The current capitol was built in 1917 at a cost of $7.25 million. The building has 2,782 steps, 705 rooms, and 1,608 doors. It was constructed using 43 varieties of stone from around the country and the world.

The capitol also is home to numerous fossils embedded in the stone. The structure has eight types of fossils preserved for all to see. None of the fossils in the capitol came from Wisconsin. Instead, the fossils were in the limestone and marble that originated from quarries in Missouri, Minnesota, Illinois, Tennessee, and as far away as Italy and France.

If you know where to look, the fossils are all over the capitol—on the walls, steps, floors, and railings. One of the most significant fossils is located in the North Hearing Room on the Second Floor of the North Wing. This room is usually vacant, and you can walk right in. Look on the back wall of this room for a view of an ammonoid, a type of extinct cephalopod. After you spot this one, look around the room for dozens more on the walls. And this is just one room.

The rarest of the fossils is a starfish located on the right side of the grand staircase, the fourth step from the bottom. Geologists say it's about 400 million years old.

Top: *Aerial photo of the Wisconsin State Capitol. Photo courtesy of Tim Manus Photography.* Inset: *One example of a fossil found on the stairs in the state capitol.*

WISCONSIN STATE CAPITOL

WHAT: Fossil hunting in the Wisconsin State Capitol

WHERE: 2 E Main St., Madison

COST: Free

PRO TIP: The capitol is laid out with four wings like the points on a compass, with the street level being ground level. You can pick up a fossil-hunting map at the capitol information desk, located in the rotunda on the ground level.

Take a free guided tour of the Wisconsin State Capitol. Tours depart from the ground-level information desk Monday through Saturday, 9 a.m. to 3 p.m., and Sunday from 1 p.m. to 3 p.m.

DRETZKA'S DEPARTMENT STORE

Where can you find mitten clips, galoshes, and polyester leisure suits?

Opened back in 1902, Dretzka's Department Store was a fixture on South Packard Avenue in Cudahy. Now open for over 120 years, the store is more of a living museum and time capsule than a contemporary department store. You will be amazed at this place's oddities and rarities.

Before you even enter, you will notice the large windows decorated with vintage merchandise. However, you'll step back in time once you open the heavy metal door. The store has an old-grandma's-basement smell and little heat. The lighting comes from bright fluorescent high-ceiling bulbs. After a few steps, a faint "hello" comes from a hidden counter in the center of the store.

The store is full of all-new items, albeit items from the past eight decades. It's a vintage lover's paradise. I found old sewing notions, rubber galoshes, white loafers, baggy underwear, Christmas decor from the '50s, men's dress socks, wide-lapel suits, and women's slacks. The list goes on and on. If you imagine what would be in a department store through the ages, there is a good chance you will find it here. I found an item I had been talking about for years. When I was a kid, I had elastic mitten

DRETZKA'S DEPARTMENT STORE

WHAT: A quirky old department store

WHERE: 4746 S Packard Ave., Cudahy

COST: Free, but you will find something that sparks a memory and you will have to have it.

PRO TIP: Be sure to stop and chat with the clerk behind the counter; it's like getting a history lesson in retail.

Left: *If you require a 1960s or 1970s leisure sport coat, Dretzka's is the place.*
Right: *Walk through the front door into a world from the past.*

clips for my jacket so I wouldn't lose yet another pair. Dretzka's had some. All items are available for purchase, and you will likely find something you can't live without.

Look up and see the cash movement system that runs along the ceiling. Clerks once sent money up to the cash office for change instead of using cash registers.

A PIECE OF RUSSIA IN MANITOWOC

What is falling from the sky in Manitowoc?

In the early morning hours on September 5, 1962, officers Marvin Bauch and Ronald Rusboldt were patrolling quiet Manitowoc when they heard reports of something in the middle of North 8th Street at the intersection of Park Street. The object was embedded three inches in the pavement near the center line. The object was too hot to touch, so the men kicked it to the side of the road and left it. The officers thought the thing was metal from the local manufacturing plant that had fallen off a truck. Following patrol, when they returned to the station, they heard a search had been called for a fallen Soviet satellite and realized what they may have found. They returned to the scene and retrieved the debris.

The object turned out to be a 20-pound piece of the 5-ton Soviet Sputnik IV satellite that had broken up over Wisconsin and fallen to the ground. First, the metal was sent to Smithsonian Astrophysics in Massachusetts for confirmation that it was part of the satellite. Next, scientists were sent to Manitowoc and surrounding areas to look for smaller pieces that may have also fallen to earth.

The original space junk was eventually sent back to Russia, and a life-size replica of the metal is now housed in the Rahr-West Art Museum in Manitowoc. The actual crash site has been marked with a metal ring embedded in the pavement. The crash site is located in the dead center of 8th Street, just a few feet north of its intersection with Park Street.

Look for the metal ring near the center line just north of the intersection, but be careful: traffic can be heavy on the road.

Left: *Manitowoc Police officers recovered the most significant piece of space junk in 1962.* Right: *The ring in the center of the road is where Sputnik IV junk crashed.*

The town of Manitowoc holds a quirky space-themed festival called Sputnikfest every year that includes a Ms. Space Debris Pageant and Cosmic Cake competition.

SPUTNIK CRASH SITE

WHAT: A piece of Sputnik IV that broke apart and crashed on reentry

WHERE: The intersection of N 8th and Park Sts. in Manitowoc

COST: Free

PRO TIP: The museum to the west of the intersection houses the replica of the debris.

WATCH OUT FOR FLYING CABBAGE

Is it a bird, a plane, or is it cabbage?

Known for cabbage and sauerkraut, Shiocton and nearby Bear Creek grow and process more of these foods than anywhere else. The Great Lakes Kraut Company has been doing business in this area since brothers Dave and Henry Flanigan started making sauerkraut in 1900.

Annually, around the first Saturday in October, cabbage lovers come together to hurl cabbages through the air. The goal of the cabbage-chucking contest is simple: chuck a cabbage head the farthest distance. This can be done in one of two ways: an air cannon or a trebuchet. An air cannon uses compressed air to launch cabbages with great force. A trebuchet is a medieval weapon that uses traction and counterweights to send items flying from a sling. There are 11 categories for the chucking events, and some are just for the under-18 crowd so the entire family can enjoy the fun.

The cabbages are all donated and must be between 6 and 10 pounds, which seems pretty large for a cabbage. However, as the cabbages fly through the air it's as if they are going through a food processor, essentially transforming into shredded coleslaw before your eyes.

ANNUAL WORLD CHAMPIONSHIP CABBAGE CHUCK

WHAT: A cabbage-tossing competition

WHERE: N5684 Lake Park St., Shiocton

COST: $3 per person, under 16 free

PRO TIP: During the chucking, the Shiocton Air Force flies over, releasing a barrage of toy soldiers onto the unsuspecting crowd of cabbage-chuckers. Some of the toy soldiers may be carrying $100 bills.

A cabbage has to be between six and 10 pounds to qualify for the cabbage chucking contest.

Suppose you are hungry from watching the chucking. In that case, the festival serves up a delicious pulled pork sandwich with, of course, coleslaw on the top.

Not interested in chucking the vegetable? Join in on one of the other enjoyable events, including a largest-cabbage contest, live music, and a raffle—and don't forget the food.

GLIDING ON THE WATER

Where can someone find canoe memorabilia?

To make seating in their canoe more comfortable, one person removed the legs of an old wooden chair, then attached the remainder of the chair to a bottom of the canoe. Inside another canoe, wood slats create a backrest that resembles the back half of an Adirondack chair, where the captain guides the sailing vessel. The Wisconsin Canoe Heritage Museum holds many beautifully restored canoes like these, along with other exhibits that perform a spectrum of different functions. From birchbark to a Rob Roy style, you can find an assortment of unique and historical canoes at the Wisconsin Heritage Canoe Museum.

Adjacent to the museum, a state-of-the-art 2,500-square-foot workshop is used for restoration and canoe-building classes. When the United States Forest Service (USFS) needed a canoe restored back to its original condition for an exhibit in their new museum, they chose the Wisconsin Canoe Heritage Museum. The National Museum of Forest Service History in Missoula, Montana, is scheduled for completion in 2025. The Shell Lake wood and canvas canoe was purchased in 1968 at a surplus sale from the Superior National Forest. After restoration, the canoe will be displayed in the National Conservation Legacy Center.

On the Saturday of Memorial Day weekend, the Wisconsin Canoe Heritage Museum holds its Canoe & Wooden Boat Show to mark the beginning of paddling season. Exhibitors bring classic and modern watercraft in all forms, along with various

---

Near Spooner, the Shell Lake Boat Company built canoes specifically for the USFS. Rangers often used canoes for timber management, to connect with visitors, and for fire crews.

Left: *Canoes can be modified and have somewhat comfy seats.* Right: *The workshop where canoes are restored.*

vintage and modern paddling-associated items. Enjoy food and music in the beer garden during the event and participate in a silent auction.

WISCONSIN CANOE HERITAGE MUSEUM

WHAT: Museum dedicated to the craft of wooden canoes and their restoration

WHERE: 312 N Front St., Spooner

COST: Suggested donation of $4 for adults, $2 for teens, free for kids

PRO TIP: To visit by appointment, call 715-635-2479.

WORLD WAR II BROUGHT THE GERMANS TO WISCONSIN, BUT NOT BY CHOICE

Why were there more than 20,000 Germans housed around Wisconsin during World War II?

One-third of the population of Wisconsin during the war years was of German descent, with many still speaking the native language. Military leaders, upon realizing this, looked to Wisconsin as a place to hold German prisoners of war. The main POW facility was set up at Camp McCoy, and 36 branch camps were set up across the state. German POWs were to be used as agricultural laborers in areas that were losing crops due to a labor shortage.

During the war, so many young local men had been drafted into the service that there was a severe labor shortage across Wisconsin, especially in agriculture. As a result, in 1945, a POW camp for Germans was established at the former Civilian Conservation Corps camp just outside Rhinelander. Just like the 34 other camps, the sole purpose of the Rhinelander camp was agricultural labor.

Most of the 90 prisoners held at Camp Rhinelander were between 18 and 23 years old. Prisoners at the Rhinelander camp woke at 4:30 a.m., had breakfast, then were loaded into trucks and driven to area farms to pick potatoes. Farmers acted as guards and were given strict instructions on behaving

---

Over 425,000 German POWs were housed in 700 camps across the United States during the war.

The POWs spent much of their time picking potatoes in Northern Wisconsin.

around the POWs. No visitation or fraternization was allowed.

The Rhinelander POW camp had no significant incidents, and it quietly closed after the war. The German POWs were repatriated in 1946. The POWs had forged long-lasting friendships with the farmers and remained in touch. Some eventually returned to Wisconsin and became citizens of the state they had become so fond of.

GERMAN POW CAMP

WHAT: Place where German POWs were housed

WHERE: The former CCC camp outside of Rhinelander

COST: Free

PRO TIP: Visit Pioneer Park in Rhinelander to see a CCC barracks like those the POWs would have lived in and learn about the impact of the CCC on Rhinelander and Wisconsin.

CROKICURL

Croki what?

When Altoona Parks and Recreation Manager Debra Goldbach searched for new outdoor winter recreation ideas to involve the community, she found crokicurl. This ice-cold new sport started to spread across Canada like wildfire in 2017. Crokicurl originated in Winnipeg when coworkers Liz Wreford and Leanne Muir brainstormed ideas about combining curling and crokinole, a popular Canadian board game.

Goldbach discussed crokicurl with Altoona City Administrator Mike Golat, who quickly took the lead. Golat swiftly formed a team to build the nation's first rink and established the United States Crokicurl National Championship, with the inaugural match held on February 13, 2021. Additionally, two leagues were established for families and adults.

As in curling, participants slide stones across a sheet of ice into red- and blue-painted center circles. More points are awarded for the stones that end up closest to the center. Unlike curling, the game is played on an octagon-shaped ice sheet with four quadrants and a bucket in the center for stones to drop into. Instead of heavier curling stones, smaller junior curling stones

CROKICURL

WHAT: Winter outdoor game played on ice

WHERE: River Prairie Center, 1445 Front Porch Pl., Altoona

COST: Free

PRO TIP: Crokicurl is for all ages and abilities and doesn't require any special equipment. Just show up.

Crokinole is played on a round wooden board with round discs. Players flick their discs across the board, trying to get them to land on high-scoring areas.

Top: *A winter Crokicurl rink in River Prairie Park, Altoona.* Bottom: *Most Crokicurl leagues play under lights at night. Photo courtesy of Tim Manus Photography.*

are used. Metal poles, used as obstacles, encircle the center, adding to the game strategy. Crokicurl is played with two teams simultaneously playing against each other. A team can have one or two people playing with four stones per team, with each team taking turns in a clockwise direction.

FRED SMITH, PICASSO OF THE PINES

Loggers, animals, Sacajawea, and a president. Why?

Nobody really knows why Fred Smith started crafting cement figures back in 1948 other than that is the year he retired from his career as a lumberjack. He was 62 and suffered from debilitating arthritis, but once he started building, he couldn't stop. One by one he crafted life-size and larger-than-life sculptures depicting people, animals, and historical events from concrete, glass, and stone.

Fred felt inspired by his surroundings and his expansive, vivid imagination. He created a full-size chariot and horses after being inspired by a movie. Paul Bunyan is the tallest statue in the park, and Abraham and Mary Todd Lincoln even make an appearance. There are more than 237 concrete and mixed-media sculptures in the park. The statues don't act like statues. Instead, Fred depicts them as attending a wedding, riding horses, drinking beer, and taking pictures.

The last statue Fred Smith made was of the Budweiser Clydesdales. In 1964, he had a stroke that left him in a nursing home. He died in 1976. Nobody ever really knew why he made the statues—not even Fred himself.

One of the larger pieces of Fred Smith's art on display in the concrete park.

Smith used concrete, glass, and whatever materials were available to him.

The statues and house were purchased and restored by the Kohler Foundation and are now managed by the Friends of Fred Smith. In addition, Fred Smith's property is now a Price County park open to visitors daily.

WISCONSIN CONCRETE PARK

WHAT: Price County park

WHERE: N8236 State Hwy. 13, Phillips

COST: Free. Donations appreciated.

PRO TIP: Much of the glass in the statues comes from Rhinelander beer bottles.

Artist-built environments are common in the upper Midwest, especially in rural Wisconsin. Often the artists are immigrants living in their new country on small farms.

ROCK AND ROLL IN THE HOUSE

Like a rolling stone?

The new floral wallpaper looked wonderful in Maxine Anderson's bedroom; it really updated the older house she shared with her husband. Standing in the kitchen, admiring the design, she heard a loud noise and crashing, and the next thing she saw was a colossal stone the size of an SUV coming through the back wall of her bedroom.

On April 24, 1995, a 55-ton boulder broke loose from the hill behind the Anderson home and rolled down the incline right through the back wall and into the couple's bedroom, where it stopped. The boulder left the bedroom in shambles, but the rest of the house was unscathed. The bathroom, next to the bedroom, even had the medicine bottles still in place. The stone was meticulous in its destruction, almost like it was premeditated.

The Andersons don't live in the house any longer, and the last owners left the house in the same condition. So now, if you stop by, the back is still open, and you can walk right in. The house looks the same way it did in 1995, the day the rock rolled in: stuff on the kitchen counter, furniture in place, books on the side table, and soap and towels in the bathroom.

ROCK IN THE HOUSE

WHAT: A house with a large rock inside

WHERE: 440 N Shore Dr., Fountain City

COST: Free

PRO TIP: The house was designated an object of unique character by the Fountain City Council and granted a historical preservation permit.

The famous House on the Rock is a mere 137 miles away in Spring Green.

That's quite a rolling stone.

Visitors can stop, walk around, and admire the large boulder. Then they can wander inside and take a step back to 1995 when the rock rolled in. Then they can step back outside, look up the hill, and wonder when the next boulder will break free and start its menacing roll.

THE *COLSAC III* AT YOUR SERVICE

Where can your vehicle take a boat ride?

Driving along Wisconsin Highway 113, you expect to encounter a bridge over the Wisconsin River. Instead you are met with an old-fashioned ferry. The ferry transports vehicles from Okee on the east bank to Merrimac on the west bank. The ferry is open 24 hours a day, seven days a week, except from 9 a.m. to 10 a.m. on Wednesday mornings, when it refuels. The season runs from April to November.

MERRIMAC FERRY

WHAT: Merrimac car ferry that crosses the Wisconsin River

WHERE: Wisconsin Hwy. 113 in the town of Merrimac or Okee

COST: Free, ice cream cone extra

PRO TIP: Ice cream and snack stands are on either side of the river, so while you wait, have a cone.

The ferry's history started long before Wisconsin was even a state. The second known settler of the village of Merrimac founded the ferry in 1844. Chester Mattson charged 35 cents per person or one dollar to ferry a team of horses and a wagon across the Wisconsin River. The wooden ferry was powered by brute muscle until the gas engine was added around the turn of the century. Then, in 1933, the state of Wisconsin took control of the ferry and made all passages free of charge.

The current ferry can carry 15 cars and is called the *Colsac III*. It was put into service in 2003.

The ferry is a cable ferry, which means there are three cables under the water attached to the ferry that winch it across the river.

Left: *The auto line waiting to board the Merrimac Ferry.* Right: *Aerial view of the* Colsac III. *Photo courtesy of Tim Manus Photography*

The Merrimac Ferry is Wisconsin's only free ferry and the only ferry left on the Wisconsin highway system.

The one-way trip takes seven minutes, and the ferry can carry up to 1,200 vehicles daily. During the peak month of August there can be up to 60 cars waiting for their turn on the ferry. A yearly season sees more than 250,000 vehicles. The ferry has survived due in part to the nostalgic feeling. Many reminisce about having an ice cream cone while waiting for the ferry on a hot summer day.

With ice cream stands on both sides of the river, most waiting for the ferry enjoy a cone.

SAUSAGE RESPECT

What is the proper way to eat a brat?

People worldwide eat bratwurst, but in Sheboygan, wherever brats appear, a social celebration follows. Although most sausage lovers, even in Wisconsin, improperly use a long, stubby bun to hold their sausage, that's the wrong way to eat them. Inside the Sheboygan city limits, a round, hard roll must encompass sizzling sausages. Otherwise, it's considered a travesty by the townsfolk. And they should know. After all, Sheboygan is the "Bratwurst Capital of the World."

In the early 1800s, German immigrants began settling in the area. One of their best-known legacies, sausage making, prevails throughout the region. Major sausage brands, along with local meat markets, continue this tradition.

In the city limits, the only way you can order a brat is on a split, round, hard roll called a semmel, with brown mustard and onions. Instead of a single, do like the townspeople do and order a double, which consists of two brats on a sandwich. Ask the locals. Nowhere in town can anyone find a hot-dog-like bun at a restaurant. In Sheboygan, cooking brats is always called a brat fry, never grilling. This doesn't mean that they're cooked in oil; instead, sausages are carefully cooked to perfection on a flattop grill or outside over hot coals without splitting the casing. When the casing splits, juices and most of the flavor are lost.

To preserve the sausage's integrity, take the Sheboygan Brat Oath. From frying, serving on a hard roll, and correct preparation, follow the oath for culinary fidelity.

Left: *People of Sheboygan love their brats so much that they have become the Bratwurst Capital of the World.* Right: *A brat is eaten on a round hard roll instead of a sausage bun in Sheboygan. Photos courtesy of Visit Sheboygan*

Each summer, brats are celebrated at Johnsonville Brat Days. Events like the Brat Trot Run, a brat-eating contest, a parade, and free entertainment occupy event-goers as thousands of pounds of sausages fry golden brown all the way around.

THE PROPER WAY TO EAT A BRAT

WHAT: Sausage misconceptions

WHERE: Sheboygan

COST: Varies

PRO TIP: Cook and turn brats by hand without using tongs or utensils. Squeezing a sausage with fingertips can help you determine when it is fully cooked. A soft, spongy feel means it's not ready yet. Wait for a solid feeling.

SEVEN BRIDGES TO THE END

Is this a road or a trail?

Hidden within the Van Loon Wildlife Area is a group of seven bridges whose architecture is some of the last of its kind in the country. Five of these bridges are listed on the National Register of Historic Places. The rare bowstring truss bridges were built between 1905 and 1908. As the story goes, in the early 1850s a Scottish immigrant created a small settlement and ferry service over the Black River. For the next 40 or so years, Alexander McGilvray's ferry service made seasonal river crossings. However, local residents needed a more reliable way to cross the river, and in 1892, the county erected wooden bridges. Unfortunately, the many floods along the marshy river rotted the wooden bridges and made them unusable. So along came La Crosse Bridge and Steel Company, which built a series of steel bridges. These bridges had a bowstring arch truss and incorporated hook clips instead of rivets.

SEVEN BRIDGES TRAIL

WHAT: McGilvray Road Seven Bridges Trail

WHERE: N8327 Amsterdam Prairie Rd., Holmen

COST: Free

PRO TIP: Parking is limited, so plan ahead. There are a few picnic tables near the parking lot. We were there in the winter, which was relatively peaceful. It's an excellent place to walk a dog.

The longest bowstring arch truss bridge still being used is in Decorah, Iowa. It is 156 feet long and was built in 1879.

Left: *The story of the bowstring bridges in McGilvray Park.* Right: *A bowstring bridge spans a river.*

A nonprofit group has been working for years to restore the bridges and has done an excellent job. In 1997, the group brought in a bridge from Pierce County and added it to the trail system.

The bridges are located along what used to be McGilvray Road. The road is closed to vehicular traffic but has been turned into a trail. The trail runs 3.8 miles and is considered an easy route. Wildlife is plentiful along this path, with over 100 species of birds. Raccoons, deer, beavers, snakes, and amphibians are also abundant.

A SHRINE BUILT FROM WHATEVER

Missing the ball from the top of your stick shift?

Dickeyville is home to what some would call either a religious monument or folk art.

Between 1920 and 1930, a German American priest was pastor at Holy Ghost Parish in Dickeyville. He dedicated his life to the unity of two great American ideals: love of God and love of country. To show his dedication, he created a monument. The Dickeyville Grotto and shrines were built from materials collected from around the world. The grotto includes colored glass, gems, pottery, porcelain, stalagmites and stalactites, seashells, starfish, petrified sea urchins, and fossils. Other materials included corals, amber, agate, quartz, ores, gold, and petrified wood. The artist also included a somewhat quirky material: numerous round stick-shift toppers from old cars are embedded throughout the structures. Father Matthias Wenerus never worked with a blueprint; he just built as he felt with materials he found.

DICKEYVILLE GROTTO

WHAT: Religious grotto

WHERE: 255-377 Great River Rd., Dickeyville

COST: Free, with donation boxes

PRO TIP: Clean restrooms and a lovely gift shop are on the premises.

The property has lots of benches, so be sure to take a seat and listen to the sound of the wind blowing through the natural contours of the grotto.

The complex consists of several shrines in the grotto garden. Besides the main shrine, there is a patriotic shrine, the Sacramental Shrine of the Holy Eucharist, the Sacred Heart Shrine, the Christ the King Shrine, the Fatima Shrine, and the Stations of the Cross. All the shrines are located in a beautiful floral garden area. The main cave houses the Grotto of the Blessed Virgin.

From inside one of the shrines, you can see all the different materials that were used in the construction.

The main entrance to the Dickeyville Grotto.

THE KING OF KARATE

What would you do?

As the story goes, around 1 a.m. on June 24, 1977, Elvis Presley arrived at the airport in Madison for a concert at Dane County Coliseum. While Elvis rode down Stoughton Road in his limo, the car stopped at a red light at the intersection of East Washington Avenue and Stoughton Road. Looking out the limo window, Elvis noticed a worker at the Skyland Service Station being harassed by two teenage boys. Asking the driver to wait and see what happened when the three started fighting, Elvis, still in his sequined blue jumpsuit from a Des Moines concert a few hours earlier, immediately jumped out of the limo and ran to the aid of the gas station worker, kicking karate-style and yelling, "I'll take you two on." After a few classic karate moves by Elvis, who earned his eighth-degree black belt in 1974, the teens recognized him, stood, and shook hands. They then promised Elvis they would stop fighting. Unfortunately, the teens were so rattled they didn't even bother to get an autograph. They should have, because Elvis died 52 days later at his home in Memphis.

ELVIS FIGHT

WHAT: Elvis Fight historical marker

WHERE: 3618 E Washington Ave., Madison (located to the left of the corner, next to the sidewalk)

COST: Free

PRO TIP: Traffic is quite busy on the corner of East Washington Avenue and Highway 51, and there isn't any parking. Find a side street to park along and walk to the marker.

Elvis performed eight times in the state of Wisconsin, with his first time being in 1956 in La Crosse.

Elvis memorial on the corner of Highway 51 and East Washington Avenue in Madison.

The service station has been closed for years, and there is currently a car lot on the site. Hidden under some bushes on this bustling corner is a stone monument marking the event from a hot summer night in 1977.

OUTFIT YOUR LIFE WHILE EATING KETTLE CORN

What do canvas, bedding, jackets, and kettle corn have in common?

Lands' End has been a staple in the small town of Dodgeville for as long as I can remember. I even worked as a customer service order-taker in high school in the '90s, as did many of my friends. Many of us grew up wearing their clothes, sleeping on their sheets, and carrying our books and goods in their canvas bags. Lands' End is Dodgeville and southwestern Wisconsin.

However, unknown to many is the Lands' End warehouse clearance sale. Every year around the first weekend in August, Lands' End takes over Harris Park in Dodgeville for a six-day event. Here you will find amazing deals, up to 75 percent off a vast assortment of Lands' End products. Tables and clothing racks are continuously stocked throughout the day with overstock, samples, and returns. Everything you would find online or in their print catalog is available at the sale at deep discounts. While browsing, listen for the specials of the hour to save even more.

The sale runs from 7 a.m. or 8 a.m. until 8 p.m. most days and is under the cover of the Ley Memorial Pavilion, so the weather is not an issue. You will spend a big chunk of your day digging through the deals, but not to worry—concessions are on-site. Also, check out the local Boy Scout kettle corn stand outside the sale; it will make your tongue sing.

The sale runs six days and is discounted even further each day. Therefore, the last day may have a different variety and assortment than the first day, but the discounts will be the greatest.

Dodgeville's Ley Pavilion is stuffed with boxes and boxes of new Lands' End merchandise.

Come early to the sale for the best selection and then again on the event's last day when everything is offered at an additional discount.

LANDS' END WAREHOUSE SALE

WHAT: Yearly Lands' End warehouse clearance event

WHERE: Harris Park Ley Pavillion, 598 N Bennett Rd., Dodgeville

COST: Free, but come prepared to shop!

PRO TIP: At the entrance to the sale, pick up a free garbage bag to carry your loot around the large sale. Shopping carts are not provided.

TRAVEL THIS BRIDGE DURING THE DAY

Have you checked your back seat?

Stevens Point has more haunted places than most towns in Wisconsin, and the most infamous is along Highway 66 northeast of town. Near Jordan County Park is a relatively low-profile bridge over the Plover River, and according to folklore, the site of a horrific event.

According to the lore, a bride was killed in an accident when her car veered off the bridge at this location on her wedding night. A police officer driving the dark road first encountered the ghostly apparition. While he was crossing the small bridge, the bride appeared in front of his patrol vehicle. The officer slammed on his brakes and thought he had hit her. He got out of his car to investigate and found nothing. Still shaking from the encounter, the officer got back in his car. As he looked in the rearview mirror, he locked eyes with the bloodied bride in his back seat. As he started to drive to take her to the hospital, she vanished just the way she had appeared.

BLOODY BRIDE BRIDGE

WHAT: A haunted bridge

WHERE: Intersection of Highway 66 and County Highway Y, northeast of Stevens Point

COST: Free

PRO TIP: There is a nice pullout near the bridge if you would like to sit in your car in the middle of the night for a chance to see the bloody bride. You may not be alone.

Stevens Point has two additional haunted bridges, Red Bridge and Black Bridge, each with its own legend.

The bridge looks normal during the day but is said to be haunted at night.

Many have claimed to see the bride along this stretch of road late at night. Some have even locked eyes with her by glancing in their rearview mirrors while crossing this bridge. I visited this spot in the middle of the day and even then I had a feeling of hesitation as I looked in the rearview mirror. Thankfully, the bride is a night owl.

MORE THAN A SANDWICH

Where can someone eat a sub sandwich in a sub?

Whether visitors are renting a submarine for an overnight stay, entering a sub-eating contest, or celebrating the Fourth of July at SubFest, Manitowoc embraces its submarine-building history. During World War II, Manitowoc Shipbuilding built submarines for the US Navy. At the Wisconsin Maritime Museum, the 311-foot-long Gato-class submarine USS *Cobia* serves to honor the submariners who served on the vessels. Each state is allowed one city as a Designated American World War II Heritage City. Manitowoc represents Wisconsin because of its submarine-building past.

Someone can sleep on the restored World War II–era USS *Cobia* two ways: either by renting an overnight stay through Sub Bnb or by participating in the Youth Overnight Program intended for scouts and youth groups. Either way, the Wisconsin Maritime Museum coordinates the visits and can accommodate up to 65 people. Experience how USS *Cobia* sailors lived during missions that saw six war patrols and sank 13 Japanese ships.

On the Fourth of July you can attend SubFest, where everything submarine rules the Lake Michigan harbor city and Manitowoc River. Many event-goers dress in classic World War II–era attire and participate in water-related events. Watch submarines and ships scurry in the remote-control boat pond, see underwater robot demonstrations, and cheer

---

Submarine crews, often referred to as submariners, often receive extra pay because of extreme working conditions, potentially up to $1,000 a month.

Left: *The 311-foot-long Gato-class submarine USS* Cobia *docked at Manitowoc Maritime Museum.* Right: *Submarines were built at Manitowoc Shipbuilding Company during World War II.*

at a sub-eating contest. Tour the USS *Cobia* and the Manitowoc Breakwater Lighthouse. On the river, watch kayaks and stand-up paddleboards race in the day, and watch the lighted boat parade at night. Finally, fireworks end the festival.

USS *COBIA*, WORLD WAR II–ERA SUBMARINE

WHAT: Celebration of the submarine

WHERE: Wisconsin Maritime Museum, 75 Maritime Dr., Manitowoc

COST: Museum entry includes USS *Cobia* tour. $20 adults, $13 for children ages 4–12, free for kids ages 3 and under, $17 for seniors and veterans, and free for active military

PRO TIP: Cross Lake Michigan on the USS *Badger*, a car ferry from Manitowoc to Ludington, Michigan.

A BRONZE TELEVISION ICON

Why is Fonzie standing along the RiverWalk in Milwaukee?

If you were alive in the '70s, you most likely remember watching the sitcom *Happy Days* at 7 p.m. on Tuesday nights. The characters will be familiar: Richie, Potsie, Ralph, and Fonzie. The sitcom took place in Milwaukee during the '50s.

In the early 2000s, the cable TV channel TV Land was putting statues of iconic television characters from the past in cities around the country: Bob Newhart in Chicago; Mary Tyler Moore in Minneapolis; Elizabeth Montgomery in Salem, Massachusetts; and Andy Griffith in Raleigh.

They had decided on Milwaukee for the Fonz, but in 2007 they scrapped the plan. Visit Milwaukee wanted the statue to be built and raised over $75,000 to commission it.

The sculpture, made of bronze, stands five feet six inches tall, was created by American artist Gerald P. Sawyer, and was unveiled on August 19, 2008. The Bronze Fonz depicts Henry Winkler as Arthur Fonzarelli, the iconic character from *Happy Days*. The Fonz gives his

---

The statue is somewhat hidden off the road. You will need to park and walk along the RiverWalk to see it.

A close-up of the Fonz along Milwaukee's RiverWalk.

famous two-thumbs-up gesture and wears his leather jacket and jeans. You can almost hear him saying, "Aayyyyy."

The Bronze Fonz is located along the Milwaukee RiverWalk near Wells Street. The statue is always busy with admirers waiting to take a selfie with the Fonz.

ARTHUR FONZARELLI STATUE

WHAT: A bronze statue of *Happy Days* character Arthur Fonzarelli, "The Fonz."

WHERE: Along Milwaukee's RiverWalk, 117 E Wells St.

COST: Free

PRO TIP: In the summer there are tables and chairs to enjoy, and the area is lovely to just take a stroll around and relax.

THE LAND OF CREATURES GREAT AND SMALL

Where do gigantic animals, shapes, and trademarks come from?

FAST Fiberglass in Sparta, Wisconsin, has been making fiberglass figures for over 50 years. Located behind the factory, somewhat obscured from the road, is a cemetery of sorts minus the dead bodies—a fiberglass mold holding area. Pull in and park, but take note of the visitors sign warning that bee nests are prevalent in the molds. Walking through the mold graveyard is like walking through a science fiction novel set after the apocalypse. There are weathered figures, animals, and representations of iconic trademark figures covering every inch of the field. On our visit, we spotted Big Boy, Bucky Badger, whales, elephants, ice cream cones, large work boots, the old lady's shoe house, a catcher's mitt, the muffler man, and even Satan, to name just a few. Some of the molds seemed decayed and covered in weeds, but there also appeared to be a method to the madness, and the molds were somewhat organized.

FAST FIBERGLASS

WHAT: Fiberglass mold graveyard

WHERE: 14177 County Hwy. Q, Sparta

COST: Free

PRO TIP: Take time to stop in the office of FAST if it's open; the owner sells a color brochure of the field for $5.

In 2018, FAST made 85 life-size Bucky Badger statues to be displayed around Madison in "Bucky on Parade," a free public art event.

Left: *Big Boy signs were easily spotted among the molds in the graveyard.*
Right: *Relics of the past are found throughout the fiberglass graveyard.*

Think of all the large items you have taken a picture with, or posed your dog in front of, that you now may know the origin of. Have you visited the World's Largest Muskie in Hayward or the 40-foot dinosaur at the Sinclair Station in the Dells? Well, both were born in the small town of Sparta. Products of the company are scattered all over Wisconsin and the world.

PIECES OF WISCONSIN AROUND THE WORLD

Why are pieces of Neenah in front of many of the world's iconic landmarks?

If you are traveling far from home and need a taste of Wisconsin, look down; chances are good that you will see a cast-iron treasure from Wisconsin. US Army members deployed to Kuwait stepped on a manhole cover there to feel like they were back home. If you admire the Eiffel Tower in Paris, look beneath it; there is a manhole cover stamped "Neenah" from Wisconsin. Hawaii has some pre–Pearl Harbor covers. Neenah manhole covers are on Broadway, in Battery Park, and near Niagara Falls. Next time you are on a major city's sidewalk, look down; there's a good chance there is a 250-pound sign from home.

Neenah Foundry was founded in 1872 as Aylward Plow Works and manufactured cast-iron plow blades, stoves, bean pots, barn door rollers, and sleigh shoes. In 1904, the company was renamed Neenah Foundry and started making manhole covers, sewer covers, and tree grates. The factory now produces more than 750,000 manhole frames and

MANHOLE COVERS

WHAT: Neenah Foundry manhole covers

WHERE: 2121 Brooks Ave., Neenah

COST: Free

PRO TIP: There is a Neenah manhole cover in the tequila and gin aisle of Woodman's East on Milwaukee Street in Madison.

If all the manhole covers produced in one year were placed side by side, they would stretch 355 miles; that's Wisconsin end to end.

You can always tell if the manhole cover is from Wisconsin; just look for the Neenah Foundry stamp.

covers per year. Today 80 percent of the manhole covers Neenah produces go to Chicago, as they have since 1920. Chicago has an estimated 148,000 manhole covers, three per block.

When you are far from home, it is always nice to look down and see the Neenah stamp and instantly feel a sense of American pride.

FROZEN RIDE

Where can you drive on water?

When Lake Superior ice becomes thick enough, an opportunity to drive on the Madeline Island Ice Road opens up. Chequamegon Bay doesn't freeze every year, but in some winters the ice gets thick enough to drive on for a few weeks.

The Madeline Island Ferry Line transports residents, visitors, and their vehicles between Bayfield and La Pointe throughout the year until the ice becomes too thick. When ice becomes too thick for the ferry but isn't solid enough for vehicles to drive on, passengers ride in custom-designed windsleds built and operated by locals. But operating the windsleds has become costly, and kids on the island still need to attend school in Bayfield. Thus, the two-mile-long ice road became the only designated ice road on state maps thanks to state senator Robert Jaunch, who successfully pushed through a bill making the ice road a critical transportation route to public schools. He stated that if school buses get funding, then an ice sled that serves the same purpose should also receive funding.

A volunteer road crew monitors the route daily to ensure ice is safe and at least 11 inches thick. They recommend driving with your window down and seat belt off if a fast escape is necessary. Additionally, while driving on the ice road, listen for cracking sounds like shattering windows.

On March 2, 1977, Lyle Rhine from Dale Movers in Minneapolis began moving a two-story house across the ice road. Near the end, the big rig and house broke through the ice,

---

Riding the ferry starts at $30 round trip per vehicle, plus each passenger fee. Visitors on a budget can see Madeline Island and Big Bay State Park more cheaply during winter.

The ice rescue boat stands by at the entrance to the Madeline Island Ice Road. Photo courtesy of Tim Manus Photography

slowly sinking with the moving truck still in gear and the motor running. Lyle drove with the door open to jump out, just in case. To commemorate the event, a local folk musician, Tim Chaney, wrote and performed his song "It Sunk" in bars around Northwest Wisconsin.

MADELINE ISLAND ICE ROAD

WHAT: Ice road between Bayfield and Madeline Island

WHERE: Bayfield

COST: Free

PRO TIP: Strictly follow all rules for your safety. Call 715-747-5400 for daily ice road updates.

SMALL CURDS, BIG DEAL

Where do Culver's cheese curds come from?

If a regular bag of Culver's famous cheese curds weighs a third of a pound, then LaGrander's Hillside Dairy produces enough curds to make 21 million bags of deep-fried cheese curds each year. The well-known restaurant chain exclusively uses this family-owned cheese plant in Stanley to supply all of its cheese curds. Large pallet–size bins of fresh yellow and white curds ship daily to a breading plant and are then prepared in smaller restaurant-sized packages.

Although Culver's might be their most recognizable customer, great cheese starts with extraordinary people. In 1960, Dannie and Lorraine LaGrander bought Hillside Dairy.

Working alongside them now is their son Randy, who became a cheesemaker at age 15 and a master cheesemaker in 2004; the third generation includes Ryan, a master cheesemaker, and Joe, a cheesemaker. LaGrander's produces 50 varieties of cheese, specializing in cheddar, Colby, Colby jack, gouda, Monterey jack, pepper jack, and curds. Primarily a wholesale manufacturer, the factory makes cheese for brands the public might recognize. For instance, pepper jack is found in Amish and Mennonite communities under the Troyer brand, and various types are made for Sargento.

The public can purchase cheese by visiting LaGrander's cheese shop on-site. The shop is a throwback to when cheese

LAGRANDER'S HILLSIDE DAIRY

WHAT: Cheese factory that produces cheese curds for Culver's

WHERE: W11299 Broek Rd., Stanley

COST: Cheese priced per pound

PRO TIP: For approximately 12 hours after being made, fresh cheese curds squeak when bitten into. To restore the squeak, warm them in the microwave for a few seconds.

Left: *LaGrander's cheese in Stanley.* Right: *Fresh cheese curds at LaGrander's Hillside Dairy.*

factories sold cheese produced that day in a small, no-frills adjoining shop. Employees would cut your order from big horns or blocks and then wrap it in paper. However, this shop is more modern, selling a larger variety of cheeses plus locally made gifts and products. Don't forget cheese curds!

A master cheesemaker is also referred to as a "PhD in cheese." Certification can only be obtained in Wisconsin and Switzerland.

LITTLE HOUSE IN THE BIG WOODS

How did a small girl become part of all our lives?

Driving through the small town of Pepin in Northwest Wisconsin, you would never guess a famous landmark is nearby. Once upon a time, a little girl lived in the big woods of Wisconsin in a small gray house made of logs. Laura Ingalls Wilder fans will recognize this from her first book, *Little House in the Big Woods*. Laura Ingalls's family's log cabin and the inspiration for her first book are located about seven miles north of Pepin on County Road CC in a modern farming community. The log cabin may be a replica, but it is located on land once owned by Charles and Caroline Ingalls and that land is where Laura Ingalls was born in 1867. Laura and her family lived in the cabin for about two years until they moved west. However, the family returned to the house in Pepin in 1871, and the girls attended Barry Corner School just down the road. Now open to the public as a historic site, the cabin is on three acres with picnic tables and a restroom.

LAURA INGALLS WILDER'S CABIN

WHAT: Birthplace of Laura Ingalls Wilder

WHERE: N3239 County Rd. CC, Stockholm

COST: Free

PRO TIP: The Laura Ingalls Wilder Museum in Pepin is a great place to start your *Little House on the Prairie* journey. Open daily during summer.

Some of the old-fashioned events for Laura Days include pie eating, a spelling bee, and a fiddle contest.

A replica of Charles and Caroline Ingalls's cabin where Laura Ingalls Wilder was born. Photo courtesy of Tim Manus Photography

The town of Pepin celebrates all things Laura Ingalls Wilder. It has a museum, a city park named after her, and an annual pioneer-themed festival called Laura Days every year on the second full weekend in September.

A SECOND GREAT WALL OF CHINA

Is it hard to find a toilet at the great wall of china?

You have probably heard of the Great Wall of China in Asia, but have you ever wondered about the "great wall of china" in Kohler? Located on the back wall of the Kohler Design Center, this great wall of china is a floor-to-ceiling display of plumbing fixtures, including tubs, toilets, and sinks, in various shapes and sizes and a rainbow of colors. Just like stones are stacked on top of each other to form a wall, the fixtures are arranged similarly. The great wall of china takes mundane residential fixtures and transforms them into a beautiful, eclectic work of art. You will never look at bathroom fixtures in the same way again.

The Kohler family of companies opened the design center in 1985 to showcase the innovative products it was creating. Here you can take a journey through the company's colorful history and learn more about both the Kohler family and the town. Kohler was built at the beginning

GREAT WALL OF CHINA

WHAT: The Kohler Design Center's great wall of china

WHERE: 101 Upper Rd., Kohler

COST: Free

PRO TIP: Allow enough time for the Industry in Action walking tour. You will learn about tubs, sinks, faucets, and toilets as they are created. There's only one tour a day, and it leaves at 8:30 a.m. Reserve your spot by calling 920-457-3699.

John Michael Kohler got into the plumbing business in 1883 when he enameled the inside of a horse trough, attached four legs, and sold it to a farmer as a bathtub.

Toilets of all shapes and colors make up the Kohler great wall of china.

of the 20th century as a planned factory town to house plant staff. The charming village with ivy-covered walls and winding streets is something out of an old movie. The old dorm where the workers once lived has been converted into a posh resort and golf course.

WORLD'S LAST HUMPBACK

Is it a humpback or a whale?

Technically they should be referred to as a whaleback ships, but locals call them humpback ships. Manufactured in Superior, Wisconsin, in 1896 and designed by Scottish Captain Alexander McDougall, these ships were initially created to haul iron ore from Lake Superior down to the steel mills of Lake Erie and bring coal back up to the lakes. Through the years, they evolved to carry a variety of cargoes, including iron ore, grain, gravel, sand, cars, and oil. The ships were called whalebacks because of the oval-shaped steel hulls that rode low in the water when loaded with cargo. The ships' design allowed them to carry oversized freight with little draft. There were 44 whaleback ships built, and each one cost approximately $1,815,000.

In 1969, the SS *Meteor* was the last of the 44 whalebacks still in use, and she ran aground on Gull Island Shoal off Marquette, Michigan. The company decided not to repair her due to the extensive damage done to the hull. So, with the ship's history and it being the last of the whaleback

WORLD'S LAST WHALEBACK SHIP

WHAT: Whaleback ship museum

WHERE: 200 Marina Dr., Superior, on Barker's Island

COST: Free to see the outside of the ship, $12 for the tour

PRO TIP: A whaleback ship was used as a passenger shuttle for the Chicago World's Fair in 1893.

The SS *Meteor* was used as a sand dredge to obtain fill to build the site of the World's Fair in Chicago in 1933.

The SS Meteor *is the last of the whaleback ships and is permanently docked in Superior.*

ships, the *Meteor* was brought back to Superior and permanently berthed at Barker's Island, not too far from where she was built. The *Meteor* is now a museum; you can tour the entire ship. The museum also features exhibits on the history of shipbuilding and shipwrecks in the Great Lakes region.

WE ALL SCREAM

Why are these cows exhausted?

Sit in Weber's Farm Store parking lot long enough and you'll realize how their ice cream sales prop up the local economy. Sure, people buy milk, cheese, and gobs of other eatables, but everyone gets an ice cream cone year-round. Everyone.

It's fortunate that the store isn't open 24 hours a day, because both soft-serve ice cream machines need downtime to recuperate. They have to service Marshfield's 18,000 or so residents weekly. Maybe extra-large serving sizes or low prices ($2.25 for a large) contribute to the exhaustion of the cows at Mauel's Dairy, which supplies the ice cream. Flavors are limited: chocolate, vanilla, twist, and a flavor of the month. Add sprinkles or other toppings for 50 cents in a cake or waffle cone. Ultimately, the ice cream might be the best soft serve in the state. Watch the constant line of vehicles at the drive-up window for proof.

Most people shop for cheese and milk before getting an ice cream cone. Nasonville Dairy supplies most of the 80 varieties. Four Master Cheesemakers from Nasonville Dairy have earned their certificates in 18 types, in addition to the other great cheeses, so it's always fun discovering new flavors. Weber's sells fresh milk they produce and process on-site. Chocolate milk is always available, but strawberry and mint are produced at different times during the year and are a nice surprise when they arrive. Other surprises

Customers used to bring milk containers from home for employees to fill out of a bulk container. In 1959, a law changed and glass bottles became standard after that.

Mint chocolate swirl is a favorite, as you can see from the lineup.

appear as well: for instance, you might see a local strawberry farm selling freshly picked berries in the parking lot or happen upon cheese ends, cheese spreads, or locally made butter in the bargain cooler for a ridiculously low price.

WEBER'S FARM STORE

WHAT: Dairy store

WHERE: 9706 County Rd. H, Marshfield

COST: Free to visit

PRO TIP: Buy world-class cheese at low prices from the World Championship Cheese Contest held every two years in Madison.

HAVE A CHAT WITH A COW

What will a quarter get you?

The World's Largest Talking Cow towers above the eastern edge of Neillsville along Highway 10. Standing over 16 feet tall and 20 feet long, this fiberglass cow is seven times larger than a typical real-life bovine. The cow was created to represent Wisconsin at the 1964 New York World's Fair and was later placed in Neillsville.

WORLD'S LARGEST TALKING COW

WHAT: Chatty Belle

WHERE: 1201 Division St. (Hwy. 10), Neillsville

COST: Free, but she charges a quarter to talk

PRO TIP: A nice park, playground, and picnic area are adjacent to Chatty Belle.

If you have ever dreamed of conversing with a cow, this is the bovine to talk with. It has a coin-operated box that, once fed with a quarter, will inform you about her size, breed, and anything else she feels like saying in her high-pitched voice—not really what you would imagine from a gigantic cow. Visualize your joy as you stand below a giant cow talking to you. It is definitely a bucket-list moo-ment!

In 1966, a contest was held to name the World's Largest Talking Cow. A first-grade girl from nearby Loyal, Wisconsin, won by naming the cow "Chatty Belle." The little girl won a fitting prize: a tour of the local butter plant and 100 pounds of fresh butter.

Chatty Belle not only has a chatterbox, she is one. Her recordings change quite often so you will want to listen closely and often.

Listen to what she has to say; it may mooo-ve you.

Next to the World's Largest Talking Cow is the futuristic-looking building that served as the entrance to the Wisconsin Pavilion at the 1964 World's Fair. The building was moved here and now houses a small gift shop and radio station.

A PLACE WHERE YOU CAN EASILY FIND YOUR WAY

Where can you find a 700-pound globe?

If you are a cartophile and admirer of globes, the American Geographical Society Library is your Disneyland. More than two million artifacts from the American Geographical Society are housed in the Golda Meir Library on the campus of the University of Wisconsin–Milwaukee.

In the late 1970s, the American Geographical Society fell on somewhat hard times. It downsized from its sizable Neoclassical headquarters in Manhattan to a small rental office in Brooklyn. The society had an unparalleled collection but needed more space to house it. So they started a nationwide search for a suitable home for the collection. The application from the geography department faculty at the University of Wisconsin—Milwaukee was accepted. As a result, the entire library collection was sent to Wisconsin in 1978.

When visiting the society's library, the most notable thing you notice is the number of globes. They have hundreds of spheres, including one dating back to as early as 1613. The largest of the globes is a rare example of the "President's Globe." During World War II, the Office of Strategic Services (predecessor to the CIA) made the 50-inch-diameter globes for President Roosevelt and Prime Minister Winston Churchill. The globes weighed over 700 pounds and were believed to be the most detailed and accurate globes made up to that point. Roosevelt kept the globe next to his desk in the Oval Office, and it can now be found in his former home in Hyde Park. The globe

---

In the "rare room" is the map used by Charles Lindbergh to lay out the route for his 1927 flight from New York to Paris.

Home to hundreds of globes and one dating back to as early as 1613.

on display in the AGS library was one of 12 initially made by Weber Costello out of Chicago.

Today the collection at the library has approximately two million items, including maps, atlases, globes, photographs, monographs, serials, and digital geospatial data.

THE AMERICAN GEOGRAPHIC SOCIETY LIBRARY

WHAT: Geography society's library

WHERE: Golda Meir Library, 2311 E Hartford Ave., Milwaukee

COST: Free

PRO TIP: The library is open Monday through Friday from 9 a.m. to 4:30 p.m.

RIDING THE WAVES

Why is Sheboygan an international destination?

Sometimes we all need a midweek break, and a beach visit is just what the doctor ordered. Relaxing waves crash on the sand, and smiling surfers enjoy the time of their lives in Sheboygan, often called the "Malibu of the Midwest."

Water lovers and spectators embrace the surfing lifestyle on Lake Michigan. Although surfers ride the waves along much of Wisconsin's shoreline, many acknowledge Sheboygan's waves as some of the best on the Great Lakes. Between its location in the state's middle, its protruding harbor, and unique wind patterns off the lake, waves can rise as high as 10 feet tall during winter storms. On good surfing days, people from around the Midwest arrive for a day in the water. Thick, hooded wetsuits and booties help protect wave riders from ice-cold water. Furthermore, when temperatures drop below freezing, layers of ice cover surfboards, making traction difficult.

CATCHING WAVES IN SHEBOYGAN

WHAT: World-renowned surfing on Lake Michigan

WHERE: Sheboygan beaches

COST: Free

PRO TIP: Go between September and March to see the best surfing.

Much of Sheboygan's surfing culture can be attributed to Larry and Lee Williams, local brothers who learned to surf from older kids in the '60s at the Lakeshore Surf Club. Over the years, their love for surfing inspired them to start a surfing event,

---

In 2003, the surfing documentary *Step into Liquid* highlighted the Williams brothers' surfing, bringing international awareness to Sheboygan as a secret surf spot.

Top: *A surfer's sunrise in Sheboygan. Photo courtesy of Visit Sheboygan.* Inset: *Known as "Malibu of the Midwest," Sheboygan has embraced a surf culture. Photo courtesy of Visit Sheboygan*

which grew into the Dairyland Surf Classic around 1988. The Labor Day weekend event grew by word of mouth over 25 years into an international spectacle. Because of the event's popularity, world-class surfers added Sheboygan to their schedules. The Labor Day Surf Weekend event continues to draw international surfers to the "Fresh Water Surf Capital of the World."

A LAMELLA TRUSS BALLROOM

What do Johnny Cash, Lawrence Welk, and Southern Culture on the Skids all have in common?

Five miles west of Neillsville stands the Silver Dome Ballroom. The iconic ballroom was built during Prohibition and the Great Depression by the four Keller brothers. The entire construction project was completed in four years without electricity. The ballroom used a lamella truss design with bolted ceiling beams. This way, no posts, pillars, or beams obstruct the stage or floor of the ballroom. The silver dome is a one-of-a-kind building with rounded band-shell ends.

The ballroom also was built on dozens of concrete piers that raise the structure about a foot off the ground. This gave the building flexibility, and dancers reported they could dance for hours on the floating floor without getting sore feet.

Even though the ballroom is located in a rural area, the venue has played host to many iconic musical acts. First came the big bands like Duke Ellington and Glenn Miller. Then, in 1954, Count Basie appeared with his 20-piece orchestra. Next, Lawrence Welk brought his orchestra to the Silver Dome. Later, when the genres changed and country music became the rage in the late '50s, George Jones, Johnny Cash, Don Williams, and Pee Wee King made appearances. Then with the emergence of rock and roll came the Buckinghams, Southern Culture on the Skids, Styx, Foghat, and Cheap Trick.

The ballroom's name, Silver Dome, refers to the aluminum-painted roof that has since been shingled.

The Silver Dome Ballroom has played host to numerous famous musical acts over the years.

SILVER DOME BALLROOM

WHAT: Historical ballroom

WHERE: W7670 US-10, Neillsville

COST: Free to look, tickets for events

PRO TIP: Prior to 1933, the Keller brothers built a supper club with a basement speakeasy located next to the ballroom. Now called the Speakeasy, it is still in operation.

Today the Silver Dome Ballroom still hosts regional, national, and local entertainers. The structure remains almost identical to what it was in 1933, with the original ceiling, floor, beams, and maple dance floor. Vintage fixtures abound, including the circular bar, walk-in cooler, and cash registers.

PLEASE COME IN. IT'S NICE AND TOASTY IN HERE

Would you take the elevator to hell?

On the outskirts of Verona is Epic, which develops software to help people get well and stay well, and to make future generations healthier. The company has around 10,000 employees, which is almost the population of Verona itself. Epic moved to Verona in 2005 and has been growing ever since. Currently, the campus is on 1,048 acres of farmland.

The employees who work at Epic have many ways to enjoy their day. The campus is laid out like a Disney theme park with five clusters of buildings, each with its name and theme: the prairie campus, Central Park campus, farm campus, Wizards Academy campus, and storybook campus.

Would you be interested in taking the elevator to hell? Floors are marked Devil, Satan, Lucifer, Beelzebub, and Mephistopheles; push a button and decide for yourself. You may prefer to take the slide to the ground floor in the building called Heaven. You can have your dry cleaning done at the New York "sock" exchange or visit the waterfall conference room. Take the Alice in Wonderland slide into a room full of miniature furniture. Or perhaps a life-sized Grand Central Station with walk-in train cars or a moat with a drawbridge between two glass buildings is more your style.

When Madison's iconic Ella's Deli closed, the 1927 C. W. Parker carousel that had been in front of the restaurant was purchased by Epic and installed at the campus.

One of the many quirky icons found within the halls of Epic

Interested in visiting the campus? Self-guided tours are available on weekends from 10 a.m. to 3 p.m. and on weekdays from 2:30 p.m. to 5 p.m. Be sure to bring your walking shoes. The campus is wheelchair accessible.

ELEVATOR TO HELL

WHAT: Epic campus

WHERE: 1979 Milky Way, Verona

COST: Free

PRO TIP: Epic serves about 1,300 breakfasts and around 6,500 made-from-scratch lunches on its campus daily.

A STOPOVER ON THE WAY TO CANADA

Why must you crawl on your hands and knees to reach Canada?

In the mid-1800s, enslaved people were seeking freedom in the North. Some secretly passed through Wisconsin on the Underground Railroad, a network of safe havens for those seeking freedom. One of the stops along the railroad was in Milton at Milton House.

Milton House was built in 1844 as a stopover for those on the busy stagecoach route. While guests at the inn were resting after a long day's stagecoach ride, there may have been people hiding in the secret tunnel and rooms below them.

Joseph Goodrich, the innkeeper at Milton House, was a staunch abolitionist. He excavated a 50-foot tunnel between his log cabin home and his inn. When runaway slaves made their way up the Mississippi River along the Underground Railroad to his inn, he sent them through a secret trapdoor that led to the tunnel. The 43-foot-long tunnel was three and a half feet tall, forcing the travelers

MILTON HOUSE MUSEUM

WHAT: A stop on the Underground Railroad

WHERE: 18 S Janesville St., Milton

COST: $12 for tours

PRO TIP: Milton House is the oldest grout-poured structure in the United States.

Milton House, the last certified Underground Railroad station in Wisconsin that can be toured, was declared a National Historic Landmark in 1998.

Top: *The cabin on one end of the Milton House tunnel used in the Underground Railroad. Photo courtesy of Janesville CVB.* Above left: *Lots of history has passed through this tunnel. Photo courtesy of Janesville CVB.* Above right: *The Milton House was a stop on the Underground Railroad. Photo courtesy of Janesville CVB.*

to crawl on their hands and knees to reach the basement of his inn. Here they could find refuge until the next portion of their journey. Some stayed hours, while others stayed weeks. The enslaved would then head toward Milwaukee, hoping to catch a boat and head north to Canada and freedom.

A PLACE WHERE IT'S OK TO WRITE ON THE WALL

Why is this building full of graffiti?

In 1859, Aslag Anderson, a Norwegian immigrant, built a warehouse and deep-water dock that served as the transportation center for Door County. During the steamship era, sailors arriving in Ephraim would paint the name of their vessel and their arrival date on the side of the warehouse to mark their visit. It is unclear why this tradition started; maybe the sailors were relieved to have made it through Death's Door waters and wanted to celebrate their arrival.

Through the years, the warehouse has served the community in various ways. It has been a winter basketball court, a silent movie theater, and a yacht club. Currently, it houses the Hardy Art Gallery.

Today, the building serves as a cultural symbol in Door County. As with the Eiffel Tower in Paris or the "Welcome to Las Vegas" sign, visitors have photos taken by the graffiti wall to commemorate their visit. It is a popular place to propose and

GRAFFITI WAREHOUSE

WHAT: Anderson Dock

WHERE: 3083 Anderson Ln., Ephraim

COST: Free

PRO TIP: Visitors are encouraged to leave their mark on the building but be sure to bring markers or paint. Spray paint and carving are not allowed.

See Ephraim's interesting historical buildings by riding the hop-on/hop-off tram tours. Board the tram from any of the museum's stops. Free to ride.

Left: *Rules of Anderson's Graffiti Warehouse. Photo courtesy of Jon Jarosh/ Destination Door County.* Right: *The graffiti on Anderson's Dock Warehouse is constantly changing. Photo courtesy of Jon Jarosh/Destination Door County*

have wedding pictures taken. Every year tourists and visitors to Door County make the pilgrimage to Anderson Dock to place their mark on the building and have their Instagram moment. It may be considered graffiti, but the town welcomes it as long as it is done tastefully. Unlike the sailors of the past, you haven't braved harsh waters to arrive in Ephraim. So take a moment, enjoy the graffiti, and leave some of your own.

SEE HOW A LUMBERJACK LIVED

What were Sunday photos?

Discover Paul Bunyan Camp, an 1890s Wisconsin Northwoods logging camp reproduction in Eau Claire. Located inside Carson Park, the museum's buildings hold artifacts that show what lumberjack life was like at the peak of the Gilded Age.

Camps were primitive, matching the lumberjacks' lifestyle, where they focused on work, not hygiene. If they were lucky, lumberjacks bathed once a month—but they often didn't take a bath the entire season. In the bunkhouse, two loggers shared a bed with other crawling critters like bedbugs and ticks. Each morning (except for Sunday) the lumberjacks started work at 4 a.m., with a 20-minute breakfast in the cook's shanty shortly after waking. The cook brought lunch into the woods. The crew worked until 7 p.m. and then returned to camp. Following an 8 p.m. dinner, lights were out at 9. However, Saturday night entertainment became the week's highlight, as music and instruments bridged the language barrier. Young men worldwide immigrated to Wisconsin to work in logging camps. Each one brought their style of music and often their favorite instruments. They washed clothes, napped, or took photos on Sundays, called "Sunday photos." Lumberjacks built enormous stacks of logs onto horse-drawn sleds to compete with other logging camps. The loads were too heavy to pull, so after photos, they were unstacked.

Logging camps operated from November through March, when frozen ground made it easier to transport logs to rivers. Crews cleared roads and then poured water over the top to freeze.

Left: *A step back in time to a Northwood's lumberjack camp.* Right: *A lumberjack cook's kitchen.*

WISCONSIN LOGGING MUSEUM

WHAT: Historic lumberjack museum

WHERE: 1110 E Half Moon Dr., Eau Claire

COST: Adults $8, youth $4, youth under five free

PRO TIP: Museum is open from June through September, Thursday through Sunday, noon to 5 p.m.

A camp's cook had the second most important job, and their pay reflected it. The cook could make or break a lumber camp. Lumberjacks followed the best cooks even though the cooks made strict mealtime rules such as assigned seats, allowing only 20 minutes to eat, and a ban on chatter at the table. You could eat as much as you liked, but if any food was left on a plate it remained there for the next meal.

OLD BONES

Why is a ship's hull a historical landmark?

While surveying the harbor for the construction of a new marina, a crew detected wooden remains of a ship buried beneath the water under layers of silt and sand. The 1992 discovery turned out to be the *Lottie Cooper*, a three-masted schooner that sank in 1894. During this period, three-masted schooners were a common way to transport cargo between Great Lakes ports.

SHIPWRECK OF *LOTTIE COOPER*

WHAT: A recovered 1876 schooner, the only exhibition of its kind on the Great Lakes

WHERE: Deland Park, Sheboygan

COST: Free

PRO TIP: Get an ice cream cone at the Harbor Centre Marina, then see Lake Michigan from the observation tower and beach.

Built in 1876 for the Truman-Cooper Lumber and Flour Mill, the *Lottie Cooper* sailed from Pine Lake, Michigan, to Sheboygan with a load of elm lumber for the booming construction industry. Once in Sheboygan Harbor, the captain beckoned for the tug *Sheboygan* to assist with docking, but the tug didn't come before nightfall. Overnight, the ship capsized and sank in stormy waters. Five crew members were rescued, but one drowned before making it to shore. The owners of the sunken ship left it where it rested until its rediscovery in 1992.

Portions of the vessel were recovered then reassembled into an exhibit. An 89-foot section of the ship can be found displayed beside Broughton Drive in Deland Park, next to Harbor Centre

Schooners were cargo ships that moved materials and goods between ports along the Great Lakes.

The wooden wreckage of the Lottie Cooper *in Sheboygan.*

Marina. Approximately 60 ships have sunk near Sheboygan, with estimates of 12 in Sheboygan Harbor. However, the *Lottie Cooper* is the only recovered shipwreck from the Great Lakes on display.

A NATURE TRAIL FULL OF STORIES

Where can you take a hike that tells a story?

Behind the Sherman & Ruth Weiss Community Library in Hayward is a hidden gem. A 16-acre nature park with a half-mile loop trail meanders around a wetland, through the forest, and next to a restored prairie. The gravel path is level, allowing for all types of hikers and walkers, with benches along the way. My favorite part of the trail is the wooden pier that juts into the pond. From there I can see the water lilies and small fish. The peaceful, quiet walk is only interrupted by the chirp of birds, the rustling of leaves, and the croaking of the frogs. It's a beautiful spot to get out and enjoy some fresh air or walk your furry friend.

The library has incorporated a story walk along the trail, including stops to read pages from nature-based children's books. Kids will love reading along in a weatherproof book as they walk the path and learn about the environment.

NATURE WALK

WHAT: Sherman & Ruth Weiss Community Library nature park

WHERE: Hayward Library, 10788 State Hwy. 22/77, Hayward

COST: Free

PRO TIP: Inside the library is the Used Book Room, open Monday through Friday.

Hayward's first library was established by Norwegian immigrants, and the books were all in the Norwegian language.

Top: *Listen to the abundant wildlife on the long boardwalk.* Inset: *A nice stroll around the pond on the library nature walk in Hayward.*

Adults can also enjoy and learn on their walk. An audio tour can be downloaded from the library that highlights 18 points along the trail. In addition, you can learn about the area's flora and fauna from the Cable Natural History Museum. The recording changes with the season.

PIZZA AND PIPES

Where can you listen to organs outside of baseball games and church?

Fun organ music naturally pairs well with major sporting events. But pizza? Organ Piper Pizza is one of only three restaurants like it left in America and the only one in Wisconsin. Professional organists play a 1929 full orchestra Wurlitzer theater pipe organ (not to be confused with church organs) while guests, many under 10, chow down on pizza. The antique Wurlitzer organ, formerly from the Avalon Theater in Milwaukee, uses only windblown pipes and real percussion operated by pneumatic devices.

Guests enjoy requesting songs—everything from Elvis, The Beatles, David Bowie, TV show themes, and polka to current hits. Sometimes guests have fun trying to trip up the organists by requesting obscure tunes, but they rarely succeed. However, "name that tune" always pleases the crowds. Nightly organ performance times begin 30 minutes after opening, and dancing is encouraged.

Organ Piper Pizza's professional organists know how to work a crowd. Zach Frame, featured organist, won the American Theatre Organ Society's "Theatre Organist of the Year" for 2022. Frame's passion for organs led him to record a CD in 2018 using the Organ Piper's Wurlitzer. He is also an organ technician and services the mighty Wurlitzer. Perry Petta's great-uncle performed on theater pipe organs during the 1930s in Milwaukee movie theaters. Petta is also a pianist at the Pfister Hotel in Milwaukee. Dean Rosko, an associate organist, loves playing to

---

In the era of silent films, theater organs played all sounds required in a score. They saved money by paying one person instead of an entire orchestra.

What goes better with pizza than live organ music?

audiences and taking requests. Rosko is the official organist for the Brewers and Admirals and also travels the country playing at roller skating competitions. Jelani Eddington, an associate organist, has produced more than 30 recordings, and at age 13 he won the American Theatre Organ Society's Young Organist Competition, becoming the youngest winner.

ORGAN PIPER PIZZA

WHAT: The only Wisconsin pizza restaurant with performing organists

WHERE: 4353 S 108th St., Greenfield

COST: Menu has various prices

PRO TIP: When ordering at the counter, you will receive a number. Pick up your order at the counter after your number lights up on the bingo-like board.

SLIDING WITH THE PACKERS

Why do the Green Bay Packers make snow instead of removing it?

There's more to Green Bay's frozen tundra than football. Both kids and adults can have a ball snow-tubing and ice skating at Titletown, next to Lambeau Field. The Packers organization wanted a dedicated place for fans to make memories besides football games, so they developed Titletown across the street from the historic stadium.

Part of the Titletown experience includes tubing from the top of Ariens Hill, a two-story-tall and football-field-long two-lane sledding hill that opened in 2017. After riders speed to the bottom, an automated return carries their tubes back to the top, but riders take the stairs. Below the tubing hill, an ice skating track symbolizing a pond weaves partially underneath the structure and alongside the slope. Both are designed to represent Green Bay's acclaimed frozen tundra. The two-story Pavilion offers a café/restaurant, a retail shop, and equipment rental. For another frozen experience try the Titletown Ice Lounge, where the temperature stays at 23 degrees. The lounge offers interactive ice sculptures and a cocktail bar along with ice tables and chairs.

Titletown District, almost 45 acres devoted to Packers fans, includes Hinterland Brewery and the Lodge Kohler hotel.

Titletown is taken from the Packers' nickname. Green Bay has won 13 NFL championships, more than any city. A goalpost sits in the middle of the double "T" monogram.

All your favorite winter sports right in town, next to Lambeau Field. Photo courtesy of Tim Manus Photography

During warmer months, tubing and skating are replaced by a life-size football field, fitness and exercise activities, live entertainment, outdoor games, and an exceptional playground, along with events and art activities for kids.

SLEDDING AND SKATING AT ARIENS HILL

WHAT: Where to play in the snow in Green Bay

WHERE: 1065 Lombardi Ave., Green Bay

COST: Varies, but $13 will get you a daily skating and unlimited tubing pass

PRO TIP: Tube and ice skate on community night, periodically scheduled on Monday nights, for a discounted rate.

THE GREAT WALL OF CLINTONVILLE

Why is there a portion of China's Great Wall in Clintonville?

In 1908, in a small machine shop in Clintonville, the first four-wheel-drive automobile was designed, built, and driven. The first car, called the Battleship, proved it could go anywhere a team of horses could. Otto Zachow and William Besserdich formed the Badger Four-Wheel Drive Auto Company in 1910. After that, the trend started to catch on. Eventually, the company switched from autos to trucks to supply the military during the two world wars.

In the 1920s, Walter Olen traveled to China with some of the company's heavy-duty trucks. The trucks helped build the Chinese railways. Walter, the company's president, worked with Chinese leader Sun Yat-sen. The Chinese leader was so impressed he thanked the

THE GREAT WALL OF CLINTONVILLE

WHAT: A portion of the Great Wall of China

WHERE: Pioneer Park, 22 11th St., Clintonville

COST: Free

PRO TIP: Stop by both of the four-wheel drive museums, the FWD Seagrave Museum and the FWD Seagrave Zachow-Besserdich Museum, to learn the history of the four-wheel drive.

During the Cold War, the company built a truck called Teracruzer that had low-pressure tires and could launch a nuclear missile from the trailer.

Part of the Great Wall of China in Clintonville

president with a small section of the Great Wall. Rumor has it the wall was smuggled out of China disguised as auto parts.

The section of the great wall is said to be the only section of the wall ever to leave China. The section has been placed in Pioneer Park along with a unique collection of stones from around the country and the world. Where else can you see, touch, and feel stones from China, Jerusalem, Yellowstone, and the Badlands all in one place?

BLUES, CHAIRS, AND FLYING DISCS

Where is the river full of legends?

The Wisconsin Chair Company produced chairs and phonograph cabinets. The chairs sold quite well, but the record cabinets could have been more prosperous. The company came up with a marketing plan—including records with the cabinets—to help boost sales. Soon, Paramount started recording 78 rpm records in a chair factory in Grafton.

CHAIR COMPANY THAT PRODUCED RECORDS

WHAT: Paramount Records recording studio monument

WHERE: 1819 S Green Bay Rd., Grafton

COST: Free

PRO TIP: Grafton has a walk of fame that resembles a piano keyboard highlighting the blues history and the African American musicians who recorded at Paramount Studios. You can pick up a walking guide at the Grafton Chamber of Commerce.

Paramount started producing blues recordings (called "race records" at the time) in 1929. They contracted with furniture store owners around the South who acted as talent scouts and arranged for the musicians to travel north to the Grafton studio and record. Trains arrived from all over the South with artists aboard who would become legendary. Louis Armstrong, Ma Rainey, Charley Patton, and Skip James are just a few. A small, all-white, polka-loving factory town became pivotal in an influential musical genre, and Paramount Records grew into the country's most crucial producer of blues records.

Unfortunately, what started in 1929 ended in 1932. The Great Depression hit the music industry hard, and Paramount stopped recording. In 1935, the company closed its doors. It is said that the disgruntled employees who had lost their jobs

Left: *The Paramount Records Blues Trail ran right through Grafton.*
Right: *The history of the chair factory that became known for making blues records.*

stood on the factory's roof and flung the original recordings like frisbees into the nearby Milwaukee River. Although many divers have braved the waters of the river hoping to find the recorded treasures, none have been found.

> The last record made at Paramount was in July 1932 by the Mississippi Sheiks. The factory was demolished in 1938.

FEEL LIKE A KID AGAIN

Would you send your kids to a park under a highway to swing?

Hidden under Holton Street Bridge is a secret playground for children and adults alike. Offering a peaceful break from everyday urban life, this swing park makes you feel like a kid again. All types of swings are hanging from the bridge above: adult swings, tire swings, handicapped-accessible swings, and even giant swings for two. Beneath the swings is a massive bed of sand reminiscent of a beach where a sandcastle is just begging to be built.

Visiting in the summer heat would be a joy due to the shade the bridge above offers. Imagine the feeling of the refreshing breeze and the cool sand under your feet. The park is surprisingly peaceful. Even with all the traffic from the surrounding busy streets, I was amazed at how calm the swing park seemed.

Pack a book, a lunch, and childhood memories, and spend an afternoon at this hidden gem. There is a colorful mural on the back wall of the park and a green space nearby for picnics. Adjacent to the park is a river walk and running trail.

MILWAUKEE'S SWING PARK

WHAT: A swing park

WHERE: 1737 N Water St., Milwaukee

COST: Free

PRO TIP: Evenings at the park are sometimes enhanced by local music, and a quick walk across the pedestrian bridge takes you to Lakefront Brewery. This would make for a great first date or evening out.

Because the overhead road and bridge block some snow, this park is also a great place to spend a snowy afternoon.

Swings hang from the road above over a sand bed.

Parking is available next to the Water Street park and across the river on Commerce Street. Public transportation is also available and an easy alternative.

BEARS TO BRAVES

Why does Henry "Hank" Aaron have a statue in Eau Claire?

A shy 18-year-old kid left home in deeply segregated Mobile, Alabama, for his first Major League Baseball contract. After he briefly played shortstop for the Indianapolis Clowns in the Negro American League, Henry Aaron was signed by the Boston Braves for $350 a month and then sent to play for the Eau Claire Bears, their class C farm team. His professional debut came on June 14, 1952, at Eau Claire's Carson Park, where he won the Northern League's Rookie of the Year award and made the All-Star team. Originally a shortstop but not known as a great fielder, Aaron learned how to play the right field during part of an off-season of winter ball in Puerto Rico.

During his playing career, Henry Aaron moved with the Braves from Boston to Milwaukee and eventually to Atlanta during his 23 seasons in the major leagues. Atlanta traded Aaron to the Milwaukee Brewers after the 1974 season, and he retired after the 1976 season.

In 1994, tears streamed down Hammerin' Hank's face when he recalled his memories in Eau Claire during his statue's unveiling in Carson Park. The Hall

HENRY "HANK" AARON STATUE IN CARSON PARK

WHAT: Statue dedicated to Henry Aaron's major league baseball debut

WHERE: Eau Claire Express Stadium, 702 Carson Park Dr., Eau Claire

COST: Free

PRO TIP: Grab a hot dog and watch a game in summer.

Baseball writers selected Aaron with 97.8 percent of votes for induction into the National Baseball Hall of Fame on his first year of eligibility.

Carson Park in Eau Claire is home to the Hank Aaron statue.

of Famer made many friends in his brief time with the Bears. Several white families often invited him for dinner, and one family took care of him as their own child. This was the first time he experienced an environment without segregation since leaving home.

Although a Hall of Famer, perhaps Henry Aaron's most significant accomplishment was how he quietly endured racism.

THINGS LOOK DIFFERENT FROM ABOVE

How can you get above it all?

Back in the 1930s, the Civilian Conservation Corps and the US Forest Service built an extensive network of fire lookout towers around Wisconsin. Many of them were located in the former Nicolet National Forest. One such tower was the Mountain Fire Lookout Tower, located 2.5 miles north of the small village of Mountain.

The tower was built in 1935 and was the 41st lookout tower to be registered in the United States. It rose 100 feet from the ground, had a seven-by-seven-foot cab, and was made of steel. The tower was in use until 10:30 a.m. on April 25, 1970, when this station's last wildfire was called in. It was taken out of service when towers became obsolete due to newer aerial surveillance technology. The tower was later restored in 1994 and repurposed again in 2015. The Mountain tower was the first Wisconsin lookout tower placed on the National Register of Historic Places.

MOUNTAIN FIRE LOOKOUT TOWER

WHAT: A fire lookout tower that can be climbed

WHERE: Mountain Tower Rd., Mountain

COST: Free, but donations are always welcome

PRO TIP: The tower is open May through November, 8 a.m. to sunset. Visit in the fall for a spectacular view of the fall colors.

The Chequamegon-Nicolet Forest covers more than 1.5 million acres of Wisconsin Northwoods. The land is used for forestry, wildlife, recreation, fisheries, and natural areas.

The views during fall from a forest service lookout tower are always fantastic. Photo courtesy of Tim Manus Photography

Today, the Mountain Fire Lookout Tower is the only tower in the Chequamegon-Nicolet Forest open to the public for visitors to enjoy the view from the top. Once you climb the 132 steps and catch your breath, on a clear day, you can experience a 360-degree view as far as 15 miles.

CURE FOR A SWEET DISEASE

Where can you find a turtle and an opera together?

Nearly century-old candy-making equipment mixed with modern gadgets sit atop tables on old hardwood floors in a scene that looks as if it's from the early 1900s. Traditional tools of the trade, like copper kettles and wooden paddles, are still used to produce divine handmade candies from recipes handed down through generations. Joseph A. Beerntsen opened his candy store at this location in 1932. Although watching the candy-making process is fun on its own, a visit to the adjoining old-fashioned candy shop at the right time brings the smell of fresh, warm chocolate. Time for chocoholics to celebrate.

Inside the store, vintage wooden candy cabinetry holds an unimaginable amount of sweet treats on both sides of the store. Fine candies and chocolates sit inside large glass cases. Specialties include truffles (the most popular), turtles, caramels, and toffee. Glass cases also contain copious amounts of unusually shaped novelty molded chocolate: handcuffs, carpentry tools, airplanes, musical instruments, and animals, to name a few. Modern candy favorites sit on top of counters too. During the holidays, handmade ribbon candy and candy canes are favorites.

With so many treats to choose from, it's easy to satisfy your sweet tooth.

Stop into Beerntsen's Confectionary and watch the candy being made.

BEERNTSEN'S CONFECTIONARY

WHAT: Old-fashioned candy shop

WHERE: 108 N 8th St., Manitowoc

COST: Free to visit

PRO TIP: It's advertised as ice cream, but Beerntsen's, actually sells custard made fresh in the shop. According to staff, Beerntsen's has made their own fresh custard since the shop began serving it years ago.

But Beerntsen's isn't limited to just candy; they have ice cream, too. Tulip-shaped ice cream sundae glasses line shelves nestled within classic black walnut cabinetry at the soda fountain. Ordering a sundae is fun with names like Chocolate Shower, Honeymoon, Opera, Coney Island, Sunset, and Wisconsin Beauty.

Watch candy-making through big plate-glass windows from the sidewalk. On the right side, a conveyor belt promises to bring back memories of the famous *I Love Lucy* episode.

FINDING YOURSELF CENTERED BETWEEN TWO PLACES

Ever wonder where exactly you are in the world?

There is a place in Wisconsin where you can join visitors from around the world, all seeking a unique piece of ground. That spot is located 21 miles west of Wausau in the tiny community of Poniatowski. The exact center of the northwest hemisphere is where the 45th parallel of latitude intersects the 90th meridian of longitude. This spot is situated halfway between the North Pole and the equator and halfway between the Greenwich meridian and the International Date Line. There are only four 45-degree-by-90-degree locations in the world. Two are under the oceans, one is high in the mountains of China, and the fourth is located in the Badger State.

In the 1960s, John Gesicki, a local resident and business owner, started researching the plot on maps and realized this was a magical place. He eventually petitioned the USGS to mark the exact spot. Finally, in 1969, the US Geological Survey arrived ready to place the marker in the park Mr. Gesicki had prepared for the world to see.

One of Wisconsin's smallest county parks attracts a stream of visitors from around the world eager to stand on a marker in the middle of a soybean field just because of what it represents.

To become a member of the 45° × 90° club, stop by the Wausau/Central Wisconsin Visitor Center and sign the 45° × 90° logbook. You may even receive a special medallion.

Just like little Madibelle Mabel, near Wausau experience one of only four 45° × 90° geographical spots in the world

The short, level, gravel path leads you to the marker with benches and informational kiosks along the way.

CENTER OF THE NORTHWEST HEMISPHERE

WHAT: Geographic 45° × 90° marker

WHERE: 5651 Meridian Rd., Athens

COST: Free

PRO TIP: Peter and Lou Berryman, Wisconsin folk singers, even wrote a song about the spot, "Poniatowski."

A GIFT FROM FRANCE

Where can you step back in time for a Parisian experience?

In 1872, shortly after Perrier began bottling water from southern France, Paris installed artistic public drinking sculptures called Wallace fountains. Kenosha received a replica Wallace fountain as a gift from their French sister city, Douai, in 2001. In 1979, French automobile manufacturer Renault acquired a large portion of the American Motors Corporation (AMC). Renault also had a factory in Douai, so naturally, the two became sister cities. Now, the Wallace fountain sits on the old AMC factory site in Southport Marina Park but is not used as a fountain. America may have up to 10 of the rare Wallace fountains.

Made from cast iron and painted dark green, Wallace fountains were built in four styles and stand over nine feet tall. Four caryatids, or sculpted female figures, hold up the fountain's dome. Each figure represents one of four virtues (some say they represent the four seasons as well), and slight differences can be detected by how each bends her knees and the placement of her tunic. The virtues and seasons are paired as follows: kindness and winter, simplicity and spring, sobriety and autumn, and charity and summer.

In 1872, Sir Richard Wallace initiated and funded the construction of public drinking fountains in Paris because poor people could not afford safe drinking water. The Franco–Prussian War had ruined sources of clean drinking water, often making the small amount of safe water available more expensive than alcoholic beverages. Thus, the underprivileged drank more alcoholic beverages, mostly beer and wine, than

---

Napoleon III chose dark green to bring nature's colors into the city streetscapes. Morris columns, iconic public benches, and traditional newsstands use the same green.

Kenosha received a replica Wallace fountain as a gift from their French sister city, Douai, in 2001.

WALLACE FOUNTAIN OF PARIS

WHAT: Water fountain gifted from France

WHERE: Place De Douai at the intersection of 2nd Ave. and 56th St.

COST: Free

PRO TIP: Ride Kenosha's historic streetcars to see the fountain.

water. Initially, more than 50 fountains were placed around Paris. Their tall basins prevented stray dogs from drinking the water, and horses could not fit their heads between the closely spaced caryatids, thus helping to keep the water clean. Yet, two tin-plated iron cups were chained inside the reservoir filled with a constant stream of water. For sanitary reasons, the cups were intended to stay submerged when not in use.

NATURE SPARKED A NATURE LOVER

Why did John Muir settle in this spot in Wisconsin?

Many of us think of John Muir as an explorer hiking the Sierra Nevada range, the Grand Canyon, Yosemite, and the Western wilderness and protecting and preserving the lands for future generations. John Muir, however, grew up in Wisconsin and fell in love with nature on a small lake just north of Portage.

Back in Scotland, Muir's family was planning their move to the woods of Canada when John was 11 years old. However, during their six-week voyage aboard a ship crossing the Atlantic, Muir's father started to rethink his decision to resettle in Canada. Immigrants aboard the vessel were speaking highly of Wisconsin and Michigan, which sparked Muir's father's interest. Upon docking in Buffalo, Muir met a grain dealer and asked where his grain came from. When the dealer said Wisconsin, the Muir family immediately made their decision and settled northeast of Portage beside the Fox River and Ennis Lake. From 1849 to 1855 John Muir lived in

JOHN MUIR MEMORIAL COUNTY PARK

WHAT: John Muir's childhood home

WHERE: N1424 County Rd. F, Montello

COST: Free

PRO TIP: Read John Muir's 1913 memoir about growing up in Wisconsin, *The Story of My Boyhood and Youth.*

Hike a portion of the Ice Age Trail around Ennis Lake. Kiosks explain how the glaciers shaped the land and how John Muir saved the wilderness.

this location until he left to attend the University of Wisconsin–Madison. He fell in love with the prairies and woods and formed his connection to nature. Years later, John Muir would become the "father" of our national parks and founder of the Sierra Club.

Today you can explore the trails in and around John Muir County Park. The park remains in its natural state, and you can experience it much as John Muir did as a child.

The sign marks the place of John Muir's childhood.

A BOAT ON LAND

What's a yacht without water?

Hidden near the University of Wisconsin–Milwaukee campus is a genuinely unconventional house. It's not a single-story, duplex, or Craftsman-style home, but a boat. Yes, it is a house built from boat plans with no intention of ever seeing the sea. The home looks like a 70-foot-long yacht perched on a hilly grass lawn.

The home has 550 square feet of space and all the luxuries of a typical home: two bedrooms, a bathroom, a galley kitchen, a dining room, and a living room. It also features lots of porthole windows and has its own 30-foot lighthouse built off the boat's starboard. There is a lovely promenade deck that wraps around the structure. The interior is furnished with a nautical flair.

In the 1920s, a traveling salesman named Edmund B. Gustorf built his yacht-bungalow. He was a mariner at heart and dreamed of sailing the high seas. Gustorf was a boat enthusiast but was not known to be a skilled captain. He once built an actual boat, but it sank when launched from the Milwaukee Yacht Club. His ships were better on dry ground.

BOAT HOUSE

WHAT: A boat-shaped house

WHERE: 3138 N Cambridge Ave., Milwaukee

COST: Free

PRO TIP: If you want to stay in the boat house, you're in luck. It is now being rented as an Airbnb.

The boat almost set sail once in 1961 when a water main burst and seven million gallons threatened to wash it into the river.

Not the type of house you would expect to see in a Milwaukee neighborhood.

Rumor has it that he built the boat house as a tourist attraction, but when zoning laws were changed, and he couldn't charge for tours, Gustorf moved into the house.

WHAT'S THAT SMELL?

What have mail carriers refused to deliver?

It's one of many examples of a dispute that led border residents to fight for their rights. In 1935, a rural postal carrier from Independence in Iowa's territory had the audacity to refuse to carry a smelly parcel in his vehicle. The Independence postmaster took his side based on an obscure edict that explicitly banned Limburger cheese. Immediately, the gloves came off. The Monroe, Wisconsin, postmaster challenged the ruling and sent a brick of Limburger to the governing panel to aid his defense. The postal hierarchy declared Limburger cheese could be mailed as long as the smell was stifled. Disagreements over the ruling resulted in a friendly cheese-sniffing duel between the two postmasters with one of the odoriferous cheeses ever. The pungent Limburger was declared the winner.

Since the creamy white cheese contains bacteria that are also found on human skin when foot odor occurs, most agree that Limburger has an unpleasant aroma. However, a small minority of people (along with mosquitoes) love its smell. Researchers in Africa use it to attract mosquitoes for malaria research. Lovers of the cheese celebrate with every opportunity. At Monroe's biannual Cheese Days parade, you can see a float dedicated to Limburger, complete with a crowned, waving queen.

Originally, monks from the Duchy of Limburg created the cheese. Because of border changes over time, the area lies

---

Traditionalists eat Limburger sandwiches at Baumgartner's in Monroe, made with dark rye bread, Limburger, red onion slices, pub mustard, and served with a mint. Bock beer makes a perfect complement.

Limbgurger is said to be the cheese with the worst smell but also a favorite among many.

CHALET CHEESE CO-OP

WHAT: The only Limburger cheese factory in America

WHERE: N4858 County Hwy. N, Monroe

COST: Free smells

PRO TIP: In 1905, New Glarus made Limburger legal tender. Try bartering with blocks of Limburger instead of cash or a credit card.

mostly in Belgium now. In the United States during Limburger's heyday, it was one of the most popular cheeses and was produced in factories across America, including in Green County. Millions of pounds were produced and then shipped to Madison on a train called the Swiss–Limburger Express. At present, the Chalet Cheese Cooperative outside of Monroe is the only remaining producer of Limburger cheese in the country.

WASHINGTON ISLAND STAVKIRKE CHURCH

Is it a Viking ship or a church?

Follow a small, winding footpath that leads you back in time to the Stavkirke church, a building modeled after the Borgund Stavkirke church constructed in 1150 in Laerdal, Norway. Stave churches are multi-gabled structures that got their name from the load-bearing posts (staves) that support the buildings. Built in the same style as Viking ships, the Stavkirke has 12 18-foot wood staves or masts. The six-tiered roof has over 9,600 four-inch-wide scalloped shingles. Just like the ships, the entire church is built of wood.

In 1983, Reverend James Reiff dreamed of building a church that celebrated the Scandinavian heritage of the island. Working with the community, he made the dream a reality. With no instructions or how-to books available, the team set out to construct the church. An architect from Sister Bay, interested in this type of church, drew some blueprints based on the Borgund Stavkirke he had once visited. Volunteers, carpenters, and craftspeople started building the church in 1991.

The church was finished in 1999 when the steeple was completed. Today, as part of the Trinity Lutheran Church, the Stavkirke church is used year-

STAVKIRKE CHURCH

WHAT: Washington Island Stavkirke church

WHERE: 1763 Town Line Rd., Washington

COST: Free, donation box

PRO TIP: Once inside the Stavkirke church, look at the unique craftsmanship. The logs were hand-hewn with tongue-and-groove joints. Also, look for the unique ornaments hanging from the rafters. For example, a tool belt hangs as a memorial to one of the builders who died just months before the dedication ceremony, and a carved ship hangs in memory of a Washington Island fisherman.

round for special worship services and intimate gatherings. Each year 8,000 to 10,000 visitors spend time admiring the structure and finding a sense of peacefulness.

The church hosts 7 p.m. Wednesday evening services during the summer. Small weddings and baptisms are held at the church upon request. Unfortunately, the church can only accommodate 38 guests.

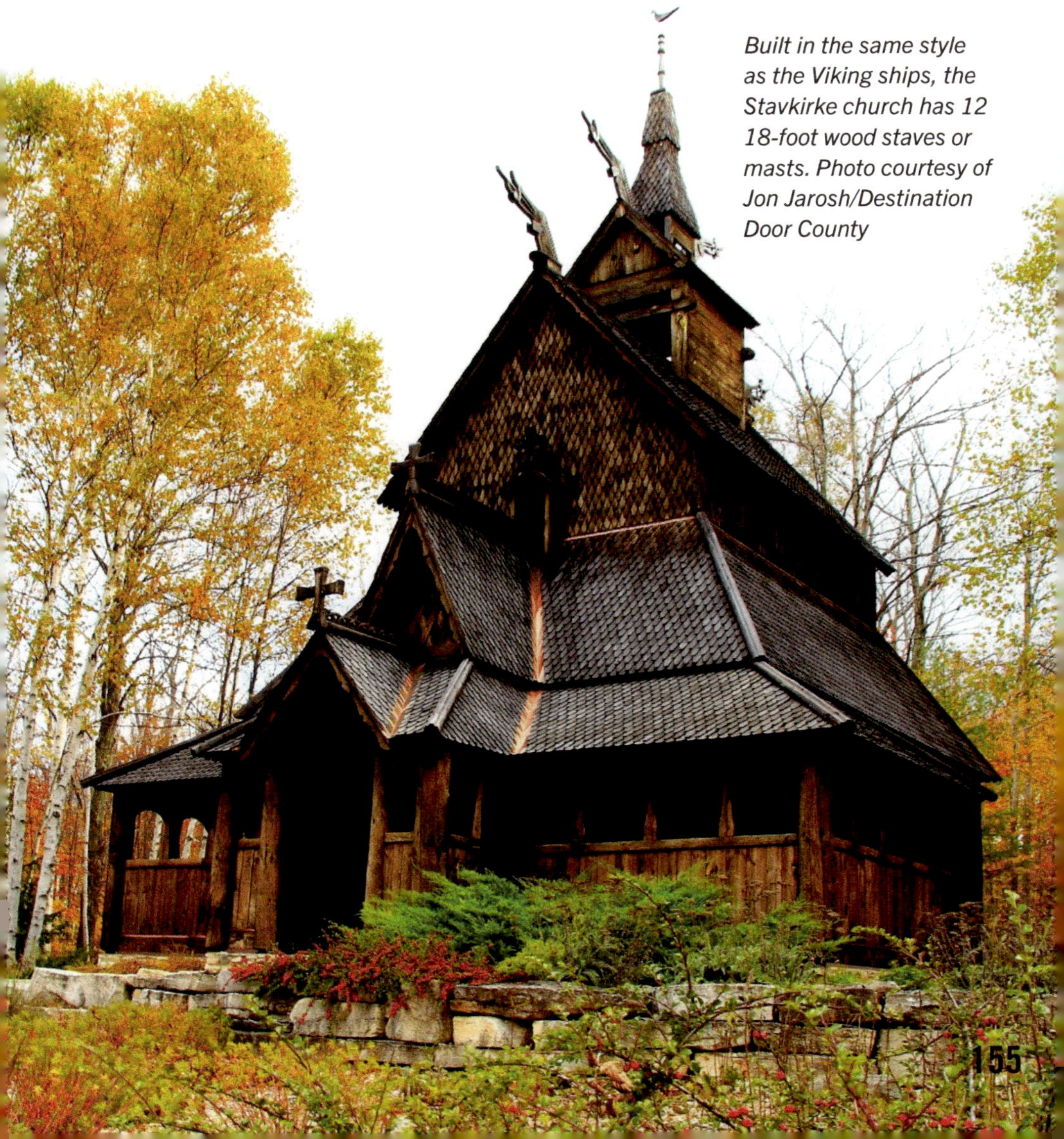

Built in the same style as the Viking ships, the Stavkirke church has 12 18-foot wood staves or masts. Photo courtesy of Jon Jarosh/Destination Door County

HONORING DECEASED POSTAL EMPLOYEES

Why does dirt from postal routes surround a flagpole?

Elk Mound might be the best memorial to deceased rural mail carriers in America. In 1934, rural letter carriers in Dunn County wanted to honor their departed coworkers, so they planted a tree on top of Elk Mound Hill and then placed soil from every rural route around the tree. They also installed a plaque devoted to the "Deceased Rural Letter Carriers of Dunn County." Additionally, a three-story stone castle–like observation tower with panoramic views sits atop the area's highest hill overlooking the town.

Visitors can pay tribute to the devoted route carriers and climb the stairs to the tower's top level. In 1937, Dunn County, with help from the Works Progress Administration, built the tower out of stones from nearby Downsville and material from a dismantled livery stable from the village. The following year, a dedication ceremony with a roll call was held for the devoted carriers who had passed. During the ceremony, the roll call was sealed in a granite marker.

While visiting the site, stay alert. Many visitors have reported hearing unexplained, hair-raising sounds like children crying in the night, screams through the trees, and sinister whispers and laughter. Allegedly, in the 1980s, someone fell to their death. In another instance, a sightseer reported being shoved from behind while walking down the steps. A family

---

A colossal dragon is rumored to be buried beneath the tower. European folklore commonly refers to dragons safeguarding riches and bodies of kings buried beneath earthen mounds.

View from above the Elk Mound Deceased Postal Workers Memorial. Photo courtesy of Tim Manus Photography

ELK MOUND HILL CASTLE

WHAT: Memorial built for deceased rural letter carriers

WHERE: Elk Mound Hill Rd., Elk Mound

COST: Free

PRO TIP: The tower can be seen from Interstate 94. Look for the flag.

member observed and verified the unnatural occurrence. Furthermore, countless people acknowledge feeling nauseated after leaving.

If you're not one to be put off by the rumors of haunting, the memorial is a great place for a pit stop. Stretch your legs and pay your respects to those who endured years of delivering mail through sunny days and harsh weather. And it wouldn't be in keeping with the postman's creed to let anything prevent a visit. Like the old slogan from the United States Postal Service commercials, "Neither rain nor snow nor sleet nor hail shall keep the postmen from their appointed rounds."

A LAKE SUPERIOR TREASURE

What is a Bayfield delicacy?

For most people traveling to Bayfield, joyful excitement builds up with each passing mile. Visitors look forward to crunchy apples from nearby orchards, heavenly ice cream cones . . . and fresh, creamy whitefish livers.

That's right. Bayfield is known for whitefish livers, a squishy local delicacy going back over 100 years. Locals tell how generations before them ate this Bayfield treat. Scandinavian fishermen who immigrated to the area in the late 1800s stewed the delicate organ in milk with onions and a dash of salt and pepper. Perhaps Victor Greunke's showmanship put them on the map in the 1940s when he began serving them in his restaurant, Greunke's Inn. Greunke dressed up battered and fried nuggets with lettuce and toast tips, then added lemon wedges and tartar sauce as garnish to win over local skeptics. Greunke freely passed out samples to diners, and many townsfolk grew fond of whitefish livers.

WHITEFISH LIVERS

WHAT: A quirky local delicacy

WHERE: Bayfield

COST: $11.95 for an order at Greunke's

PRO TIP: Don't worry about looking like a tourist. Bayfield's motto is "Real Tourists Eat Whitefish Livers."

Local fish markets sell fresh whitefish livers in quart containers of approximately 70 pieces but charge by the pound. For best results, don't freeze them.

Gruenke's Inn in Bayfield serves traditional whitefish livers.

Although Greunke's is the most popular place, many restaurants around town offer cuisine that includes whitefish livers. If you visit during the first weekend in March you can enter the whitefish liver eating contest at the Bayfield Winter Festival for a chance to be crowned champion. Get them while you can, because St. Ignace, Michigan, is the only place besides Bayfield where you can find this exquisite indulgence.

RIDE WITH US

How did a "temporary" circus poster from 1885 survive to the present day?

When Corral Bar owner Ron Berger began expanding into the space that had been occupied by a business next door, he cut a hole into a wall. He didn't expect to see a bison peering back at him—much less a colorful, nine-foot-tall-by-55-foot-long circus poster from 1885, which he uncovered by carefully removing the old wall. Berger initially intended to cut a hole in the wall big enough for a doorway to link both buildings. What was planned as a quick expansion in 2015 turned into a lengthy and detailed two-year project. Peter Schrake, an archivist at Circus World Museum in Baraboo, came to see the rare and impressive Great Anglo-American Circus poster and said it was the longest circus poster he knew of.

When circus shows were at their pinnacle, railroads carried them to each location. Teams worked ahead in scheduled towns, promoting their acts with handbills and pasting paper lithograph posters on buildings. Carved wood blocks were used to create posters by stamping multicolored images onto paper. Lithograph advertisements were the preferred method since they fell apart after a few months, meaning teams didn't need to return to remove them.

The Corral Bar's poster, stamped Monday, August 17, faces the Chippewa River, advertising to boats that passed. Running along the top, bold letters state, "ALLIE & BERNARD, TINY

CORRAL BAR & RIVERSIDE GRILL CIRCUS POSTER

WHAT: Poster from 1885 advertising the Great Anglo-American Circus

WHERE: 318 W Main St., Durand

COST: Free

PRO TIP: The Orton Room is used for private events but is otherwise empty, so check ahead of time. Mornings are best.

Top: *Circus poster from 1885 hidden behind a Durand wall.* Inset: *Coral Bar & Riverside Grill circus poster*

AERIAL MARVELS, MILES ORTON RIDES WITH US." Orton, owner, manager, and promoter, and his two young children performed while standing on top of galloping horses. In addition to elephants, giraffes, lions, and sea creatures, various circus scenes intertwine with performances and the train.

The poster took two years for experts to restore. After microvacuuming, loose pieces were repasted and then methodically washed using cotton balls and distilled water. Protective glass encases the paper lithograph.

A SELF-DRIVING CAR LIKE NO OTHER

Who says there's no such thing as a free ride?

Nestled between cornfields lies a remote county road with a mysterious yet eerie secret. About two miles south of Shullsburg in Southwestern Wisconsin is Gravity Hill, a super-fun phenomenon that must be seen and experienced to determine whether you are a skeptic.

Once you find the sign announcing Gravity Hill, stop the car completely. Put your vehicle in neutral and take your foot off the brake. Be amazed at how your car will slowly start backing up a large hill. Your car will gain speed until it is rapidly going up the incline. Feel the sensation that you are being pulled up the hill by an invisible cable, or maybe that invisible elves are pushing your car up the hill. Gravity Hill isn't a big hill, but the speed of acceleration from a stop makes it seem like there is more to the hill.

GRAVITY HILL

WHAT: A freak of nature

WHERE: Hwy. U, Shullsburg

COST: Free

PRO TIP: Try it both ways, forward and backward, for the same sensation.

Always be careful. Gravity Hill is a public highway, so obey signs and watch for other cars. Don't try this in inclement weather.

Take a thrill ride on Gravity Hill.

Many say this is probably an optical illusion or nature's tomfoolery, so judge yourself. I call it a thrill of the unknown. There is no end to this enjoyment, so skip the trip to the amusement park and head to Gravity Hill. We did it over and over again until all our skepticism was diminished.

A BUBBLER BY ANY OTHER NAME

Why is a bubbler called a bubbler in Wisconsin?

Everyone knows that thing that provides drinking water in public places like schools, malls, parks, and buildings—the thing that, when a button is pushed or a knob is turned, produces fresh, clear water, ready to be drunk. We all know it, but what we call it is regional.

Most of the state calls the apparatus a bubbler and has since its invention. One holdout is the northwestern part of the state, where they use the term fountain like their Minnesota neighbors to the west. Wisconsinites are known for the term bubbler and even get razzed about it. If you say bubbler, you must be from Wisconsin. Around the country, water fountain, gurgler, water cooler, and drinking fountain are the most commonly used terms. There are small areas in the Northeast that also use the word bubbler.

A Wisconsin original, the bubbler was created by the Kohler Company near the turn of the century. It was called a

BUBBLER

WHAT: The word "bubbler"

WHERE: Used throughout Wisconsin

COST: Free to use

PRO TIP: One of the best places to experience a variety of bubblers is the Wisconsin State Capitol. There are bubblers inside and also scattered around the grounds of the capitol. In addition, one of the original Kohler bubblers is located here.

Parts of Australia use the term bubbler, as do people in Rhode Island.

We all know what this is, but we may call it by different names.

bubbler because the small stream of water looked like it had bubbles in it. Kohler Company patented the word bubbler and promoted its trademark name. Bubbler is still being used today for its products. The name stuck and is defined in the Merriam-Webster Dictionary as a drinking fountain from which a stream of water bubbles upward.

ONE OF THE LARGEST LOONS

Where can you find the third-largest loon in the world?

Standing 16 feet tall and weighing about 2,000 pounds, the world's third-largest loon stands over the northern Wisconsin town of Mercer. Citizens raised over $10,000 to build her, and a local company donated land for her home. The loon was built in 1981 by the FAST Corporation in Sparta, Wisconsin, and transported to Mercer, where she has been ever since.

Named Claire d'Loon, she is not as agile as a real loon. She can't dive 200 feet underwater or hold her breath for over 10 minutes like real loons. Still, she can withstand numerous pictures and selfies being taken with her.

Because Claire is cemented to the ground and can't fly, she has been shot numerous times. So in 2015, locals raised money to have the bullet holes patched.

Claire d'Loon may be the third-largest loon in the world, but she is also the "World's Largest Talking Loon." When prompted, she has a voice box that gives the various loon calls and provides information about loons.

CLAIRE D'LOON STATUE

WHAT: Large loon statue

WHERE: 5150 N Hwy. 51, Mercer

COST: Free

PRO TIP: Mercer celebrates Loon Day, the first Wednesday of August. The town is filled with numerous activities on this day, including a loon-calling contest, a raffle, and an arts and crafts fair.

The world's largest loon is in Vergas, Minnesota, and the world's largest floating loon is in Virginia, Minnesota.

The loon is located next to the Mercer Area Chamber of Commerce. Claire is always ready and willing to assist you with photos and information, so be sure to stop and say hi.

Claire d'Loon towers over Highway 51 in Mercer.

A JAPANESE TEAROOM FOR YOUR AUTOMOBILE

Why was the Midwest littered with small pagodas?

Small gas stations in the early 1920s were usually bland, square, and functional, and they attracted little if any notice. Hoping to create a gas station that grabbed the attention of cars whizzing by, Milwaukee-based independent chain Wadham's Oil and Grease Company turned to an architect for help. Wadham's partnered with Alexander C. Eschweiler, who drew the plans that would be used for more than 100 gas stations around the Midwest between 1917 and 1930.

Establishing brand identity, just like Wadham's had hoped, the filling stations were attention grabbers and buildings like no others in this country. Inspired by Japanese culture, which was popular at the time, Eschweiler designed a Japanese pagoda–style filling station. Each of the 100 pagodas was unique, with different layouts. Still, all had a bright red stamped metal roof and tiered cupolas with lanterns hanging from the corners. The

PAGODA GAS STATION

WHAT: Gas station built like a pagoda

WHERE: N58W6189 Columbia Rd., Cedarburg

COST: Free

PRO TIP: There are two pagodas left in Wisconsin. The other is on South 76th Street in West Allis and is listed on the National Register of Historic Places.

Frank Lloyd Wright also became familiar with Japanese architecture at the Chicago World's Fair. He soon began using the rooflines he saw at the Japanese Pavilion.

100 gas stations around the Midwest between 1917 and 1930 looked like pagodas.

building front was all glass with yellow trim. The filling stations were meant to resemble a Japanese tearoom–style building.

Many say the architect was inspired by the Japanese Pavilion at the Chicago World's Fair of 1893. This pavilion was the first time many Americans had seen Japanese architecture up close.

Wisconsin Canoe Heritage Museum

SOURCES

We personally visited almost every location, but these are the additional resources we consulted.

Welcome to Cleveland

Stingl, J. (2015, December). "Welcome to Clevelands' sign's 15 minutes of Fame lasts 37 years." *Milwaukee Journal Sentinel.*

Traveling Egg Rolls

Nguyen, Teresa. (2020, September). "The Cozy Inn: Nearly 100 Years in Business." Janesville Area Stories.

The *Boy with the Leaking Boot*

Steven's Point Fire Department, City of Steven's Point, WI. www.stevenspoint.com.

Designed White Elephant

Feldman,M. (2000). *Wisconsin Curiosities, 2nd Edition*. Guilford, CT: The Globe Pequot Press.

How a Long Speech Saved a President's Life

Hintz, M.(2010). *Forgotten Tales of Wisconsin*. Charleston, SC: The History Press. Bie, M.(2013). *It Happened in Wisconsin*. Guilford, CT: The Globe Pequot Press.

Glass Benders

(2020, October 13). "Local Entrepreneur, Son Featured at Neon Symposium in San Francisco." *Antigo Daily Journal.*

The Battle Is Still Raging in Wisconsin

Holcomb, K.(2010). *Packing it in Wisconsin*. Lincolnwood, IL: West Side Publishing.

Turkeys in the Basement

Horne, Michael. (2014, August 20). "Hollar House has America's Oldest Bowling Alleys." Urban Milwaukee.

Otis Redding's Last Flight

Hintz, M.(2010). *Forgotten Tales of Wisconsin*. Charleston, SC: The History Press. Moe, D.(1983, March). "The Last Flight." *Madison Magazine*.

Pancakes from Out of this World

Entz, G.(2019). "A Northwoods Case for the X-Files. WXPR Radio. "Saucer, Pancakes and Such". Science. www.Science.org.

America's First Dairy School

History. Babcock Dairy Plant, University of Wisconsin-Madsion College of Agriculture and Life Sciences. babcockhalldairyplant.wisc.edu/about-us/history/.

A Businessman's Retreat

Hintz, M.(2010). *Forgotten Tales of Wisconsin*. Charleston, SC: The History Press. Feldman, M.(2000). *Wisconsin Curiosities, 2nd Edition*. Guilford, CT: The Globe Pequot Press.

Spooner Fish Hatchery

Wisconsin Department of Natural Resources: Governor Tommy G. Thompson State Fish Hatchery. dnr.wisconsin.gov/topic/Fishing/hatcheries/govthompson.html.

Working Nine to Three on the Roof

Feldman, M.(2000). *Wisconsin Curiosities, 2nd Edition*. Guilford, CT: The Globe Pequot Press.

Even Future Presidents Need to Use the Facilities

Feldman, M. (2000). *Wisconsin Curiosities, 2nd Edition*. Guilford, CT: The Globe Pequot Press.

Enter This Wild Wood and View the Haunts of Nature

Godfrey, L., Hendricks, R. (2005). *Weird Wisconsin*. New York, NY: Sterling Publishing Co.

A Night of Flames

"The Great Midwest Wildifires of 1871". National Weather Service. www.weather.com.

A Scavenger Hunt within the State Capitol

"Wisconsin State Capital". Tours.wisconsin.gov.

A Piece of Russia in Manitowoc

Bie, M.(2013). *It Happened in Wisconsin*. Guilford, CT: The Globe Pequot Press. Godfrey, L., Hendricks, R.(2005). *Weird Wisconsin*. New York, NY: Sterling Publishing.

World War II Brought the Germans to Wisconsin, but Not by Choice

Entz, G. (2019). "In 1945, there was POW camp in Rhinelander." WXPR Radio.

Fred Smith, Picasso of the Pines

Godfrey, L., Henricks, R.(2005). *Weird Wisconsin*. New York, NY: Sterling Publishing Co.

Rock and Roll in the House

Feldman, M.(2000). *Wisconsin Curiosities, 2nd Edition*. Guilford, CT: The Globe Pequot Press.

Seven Bridges to the End
"7bridges". www.7bridgesrd.org.

A Shrine Built from Whatever
"Dickeyville Grotto". www.dickeyvillegrotto.com.

The King of Karate
Holcomb, K.(2010). *Packing it in Wisconsin*. Lincolnwood, IL: West Side Publishing.

Travel This Bridge during the Day
Visit Steven's Point.
www.stevenspointarea.com.

A Bronze Television Icon
"The Bronz Fonz".
www.visitmilwaukee.com.

The Land of Creatures Great and Small
"Fast Fiberglass Mold Graveyard". Atlas Obscura. www.atlasobscura.com.

Pieces of Wisconsin around the World
"Neenah Foundry Manhole Cover". Wisconsin 101. www.wi101.wisc.edu.

Frozen Ride
Olivo, Rick. (2015, July 23). "It Sunk." Ashland Daily Press.

Little House in the Big Woods
"Laura Ingalls Wilder house." Laura Ingalls Pepin. www.lauraingallspepin.com.

A Second Great Wall of China
Hintz, M., Hintz, D.(2000). *Off The Beaten Path*. Guilford, CT: The Globe Pequot Press.

World's Last Humpback
Godfrey, L., Hendricks, R. (2005). *Weird Wisconsin*. New York, NY: Sterling Publishing Co.

Have a Chat with a Cow
Feldman, M.(2000). *Wisconsin Curiosities*. Guilford, CT: The Globe Pequot Press.

A Place Where You Can Easily Find Your Way
"American Geographical Society Library". University of Wisconsin-Milwaukee. www.uwm.edu.

Riding the Waves
Hilty, Maya. (2021, December 20). "Freezing Water, Sunny Attitudes: How and Why Sheboygan Became an International Surfing Destination." Sheboygan Press.

A Lamella Truss Ballroom

"Silver Dome Ballroom". Silver Dome Ballroom. www.silverdomeballroom.net. "Silver Dome Ballroom". Atlas Obscura. www.atlasobscura.com.

Please Come In. It's Nice and Toasty in Here

Kelly, K.(2018, December). "Willy Wonka and the Medical Software Factory". The *New York Times*.

A Stopover on the Way to Canada

"Milton House". www.Miltonhouse.org. "Milton House Museum". www.travelwisconsin.com.

A Place Where It's OK to Write on the Wall

"Anderson Dock". Destination Door County. www.doorcounty.com.

Old Bones

Klein, Gary C. (2022, July 14). "Wreckage of This Ship, On Display on Sheboygan's Lakefront, was Pulled from Lake Michigan's Icy Waters in the 1990s." Sheboygan Press.

Pizza and Pipes

Ramirez, Adriana. (2019, May 15). "Greenfield's Organ Piper Pizza is One of Only Three Restaurants Like It in the US." *Milwaukee Journal Sentinel*.

The Great Wall of Clintonville

Feldman, M.(2000). *Wisconsin Curiosities, 2nd Edition*. Guilford, CT: The Globe Pequot Press.

Blues, Chairs, and Flying Discs

Davis, T. (2022, October/November). "Of Paramount Importance". *Our Wisconsin Magazine*.

Feel like a Kid Again

"Swing Park". Atlas Obscura. www.atlasobscura.com.

Bears to Braves

Robbins, Dean; Kolberg, Brad (2012, July 7). "Baseball Legend Hank Aaron's Early Career in Eau Claire." wisconsinlife.org/story/hank-aaron/.

Things Look Different from Above

"Mountain Fire Lookout Tower". USDA Forest Service. www.FS.USDA.GOV.

Finding Yourself Centered between Two Places

"Exact Center of Northern Half of the Western Hemishere". Roadside America. www.roadsideamerica.com.

A Gift from France

wallacefountains.org.

Nature Sparked a Nature Lover

Holcomb, K.(2010). *Packing it in Wisconsin*. Lincolnwood, IL: West Side Publishing.

A Boat on Land

Freeman, M.(2000). *Wisconsin Curiosities*. Guilford, CT: The Globe Pequot Press.

What's That Smell?

Bergin, Mary. (2018, September 11). "Yes, It Stinks! But Fans of Limburger Cheese, Made in Monroe, Love it Anyway." *Milwaukee Journal Sentinel*.

Washington Island Stavkirke Church

"Stavkirke Church". Destination Door County. www.doorcounty.com.
"Stavkirke". Trinity Lutheran Church. www.trinitylutheran-wi.com.

Honoring Deceased Postal Employees

Village of Elk Mound. www.elkmound.org/content/history.

A Lake Superior Treasure

Davis, Tom. (2022, July 27). "Dumpster Diving For Whitefish Livers." Hatch.

Ride with Us

Katz, Brigit. (2019, May 22). "Huge 19th Century Circus Poster Found in Walls of Woisconsin Bar." *Smithsonian Magazine*.

A Self-Driving Car like No Other

Godfrey L., Hendricks, R. (2005). *Weird Wisconsin*. New York, NY: Sterling Publishing Co. "Gravity HIll". Travel Wisconsin. www.travelwisconsin.com.

A Bubbler by Any Other Name

Holcomb, K.(2010). *Packing it in Wisconsin*. Lincolnwood, IL: West Side Publishing.

One of the Largest Loons

"Claire D'Loon". Mercer Area Chamber of Commerce. www.mercercc.com.

A Japanese Tearoom for Your Automobile

"Old Pagoda Gas Station". Roadside America. www.roadsideamerica.com.

The *Boy with the Leaking Boot* fountain

INDEX

Holler House

Ships on the Great Lakes
Photo courtesy of Tim Manus Photography